MOB RULE

Chicago in the twenties was a city paralyzed by fear—a city brought to its knees by a scar-faced, vicious killer. Prohibition gave Al Capone a way of expanding beyond drugs, gambling, and prostitution, to dominate the entire city. Clawing his way to the top by eliminating the rival Moran gang in the St. Valentine's Day massacre, Capone made the one-way ride, the kiss of death, and the emasculated corpse symbols of an era.

Paul Robsky was one of the legendary "Untouchables" who broke Capone's stranglehold. This is the story of the early morning raids, the pitched battles in grimy warehouses, the furious mob reprisals, the men and women on both sides of the law—and the ones who played it both ways. Robsky led a violent life in one of the most violent periods of American history. He tells it with all the real-life, raw excitement of one who experienced it.

Be sure to read the runaway best seller from AWARD books that inspired the smash-hit television series:

The
Last Of
The Untouchables

by Oscar Fraley
with Paul Robsky

AWARD BOOKS
NEW YORK

FIRST AWARD PRINTING 1976

AWARD BOOKS are published by
Universal-Award House, Inc., a subsidiary of
Universal Publishing and Distributing Corporation,
235 East Forty-fifth Street, New York, N.Y. 10017.

Manufactured in the United States of America

The Last Of The Untouchables

INTRODUCTION

The city of Chicago late in the year of 1929 was a concrete jungle in which the supposedly human gorillas wore pearl-gray hats and carried their muscle in a shoulder holster.

No jungle was ever more deadly.

This was the height of a perilous period known as the Prohibition Era, a fantastically fatal age which legislative idiocy and defiant thirsts extended murderously from 1920 through 1933.

It was a made-to-order market for the opportunistic underworld. Alcoholic beverages were illegal. Premium prices could be charged for supplying them to a parched citizenry.

The first ten years, as in almost any business, were the hardest. Rivals had to be eliminated. This was done, economically, with pistol, tommygun, sawed-off shotgun and a homemade but extremely effective bomb known as the "pineapple."

By 1929 the "business" was fairly well organized.

There still were deadly "independents" but most of those reluctant to become a part of the grand syndicate scheme, some four hundred of them in Chicago alone, had been removed by the simple expediency of the "one-way ride." Mobsters swaggered through the streets, or drove through them in their bullet-proof limousines, without legal challenge because the law was in their pocket.

The nation had been marked off in rigidly inviolate territories under a network of local overlords. Chicago, with illicit liquor at high tide in more than two thousand speakeasies, was the throne room.

And its murderous monarch was Alphonse (Scarface
Al) Capone.

This pudgy man with the patent-leather hair and the
long, evil scar on his cheek—a boyhood memento from
an irate Sicilian barber on whom he had played a vicious
prank in his native Brooklyn—had worked his way up
rapidly through gangland ranks after arriving in Chicago
as the overseer of a bordello. Scarface Al had two prime
qualifications: a callous disdain for other people's lives
and a genius for organization.

By 1929 the Capone mob's income was estimated cautiously at a minimum of $120,000,000 a year. This in-
cluded income from gambling and vice, previously the
underworld's chief sources of revenue, but no less than
$75,000,000 annually came from the production and sale
of alcoholic beverages.

Then this criminal Caesar unwittingly committed two
fatal mistakes.

He arrogantly flaunted his power in the face of
President Herbert Hoover and, after a gangland conference in Atlantic City, he was picked up in Philadelphia
and sentenced to a year in prison for possession of
firearms. These incidents, two months apart, may seen un-
related but they conspired in Capone's downfall.

Capone long had owned a palatial estate in Miami
Beach and, in March of 1929, he gave a party which was
attended by various underworld celebrities and his own
upper-echelon lieutenants. At a late hour the "boys" became boisterous and staged an impromptu bit of target
practice on the premises. President Hoover, visiting at a
nearby estate, was aroused by the commotion and in-
quired as to its cause. When he was told, the President
was outraged.

President Hoover ordered that all possible steps be
taken to remove Capone from circulation.

This edict was issued immediately to the Treasury Department, already interested in Capone's undoubtedly un-
reported income, and to the Department of Justice Bureau of Prohibition.

Agents of the Prohibition Bureau stationed in Chicago had, in the preceding years, been singularly ineffective against Capone's operations. Breweries, the few times they were located, were inactive. No gangland figure of any consequence ever had been prosecuted successfully.

Thus, when United States Attorney George E. Q. Johnson received orders from Washington for an all-out legal offensive against the Capone mob, he realized that new tactics were necessary. He and Assistant United States Attorney General William J. Froelich, who arrived in Chicago to handle the case, came up with a unique scheme for importation of a hand-picked band of Prohibition agents who would be given a free hand and be accountable only to them.

The squad was formed in September of 1929, a time when Capone still had three months to serve in Philadelphia. By the time he returned to Chicago, at the end of March in 1930, the squad already was well established without any possible personal interference from him, which well might have disrupted its beginning.

The members of this special squad in two and a half violent years dried up Chicago, drained from Capone the funds necessary to pay for "protection" and helped collect tax data which led to his ultimate downfall. Through their refusal to yield to bribes, threats or violence, they became legendary as "The Untouchables."

But were they?

Paul Robsky, who was one of them, tells that true, behind-the-scenes story in these pages.

Of the three who defected.

Of the suspicions within their ranks.

Of the fears they felt.

Of the perils they survived.

Of the love they snatched in the shadow of gangland vengeance.

Robsky, a wiry man whose easy manner and soft voice conceal a coiled-steel body and a thirst for excitement, had been an aerial photographer in France during World War I, an air cadet in the same class with Charles A. Lind-

bergh, a flying Marine and a commercial flyer before joining the Prohibition Bureau. He had spent a hazardous
year in the "moonshine mountains" of South Carolina before being sent to Chicago as one of the first hand-picked
members of the band which became known as "The Untouchables."

When it ended, and the squad was disbanded for other
individual assignments, Robsky was left behind to clean
up the loose ends. This, then, is the story of "The Last Of
The Untouchables."

—Oscar Fraley

CHAPTER 1

A man does a certain amount of looking back when he is about to commence something new.

For me it all started with the teen-age lesson in my native Galesburg, Illinois, that even a low straight always beats three aces. I chuckled at the memory this rainy day in late September of 1929 as I drove the new black sedan through the waning afternoon toward still distant Chicago.

It began for me exactly twelve years earlier in the back room of the little post office at Galesburg. That was in September of 1917 and Uncle Sam was fighting a war in Europe. I was fighting the recruiting sergeant over a poker pot which must have had all of fifteen dollars in it.

He had been after me for several weeks to enlist. Now he pushed three dollars into the pot and taunted: "I'll see your dollar and raise you two."

Cautiously I looked again to make sure that my three aces were really there.

"Okay," I told him. "I'm busted out. But I'll see you if you'll take my enlistment against the two bucks."

"Done," he snapped.

Then he laid down a little old six-high straight and I, at nineteen, was in the Army.

The very next day I was on my way: St. Louis, on to Kelly Field in San Antonio and, enrolled in the aviation section of the signal corps, assigned to the 199th Aero Squadron when it opened up Love Field in Dallas.

They moved my outfit rapidly, for soon we were sent to an embarkation camp at Garden City, New York. Two weeks later we were aboard the S. S. Carmania, part of a convoy which formed at Halifax, and, after landing at gloomy Liverpool, by January of 1918 were taking training for aerial photography at Boscombe Downs, Salisbury Plains.

The car hit a bump and I recalled my second flight with an English cadet, the choking lump in my throat as he overshot the field and the breathtaking way in which we pancaked in from a hundred feet in that fragile RE-8. I was lucky to walk away from it with assorted cuts and bruises. He didn't. He was dead with a broken neck. That June, despite my limited experience, I was assigned to the Seventh Photo Section and sent to the Second Aviation Training Center at Tours as an instructor in aerial photography.

By then I was a sergeant, serial number 290,752— some 53,000,000 lower than Elvis Presley's—and had been recommended for a commisssion. My students were artillery officers who had been transferred to the air service for training as observers. However, before my commission came through the Armistice ended the war.

The next few years had gone by swiftly, I mused. I attended Knox College and then I sold automobiles. But there was a strong restlessness within me and flying remained uppermost in the back of my mind. Then, because of my service record, I was accepted as a flying cadet in the Air Corps in 1925 and it was back once again to Kelly Field.

Riding along, I thought of that period of my life with mixed emotions. I chuckled when I remembered how I had talked our shabbily clad group into buying what I envisioned as snappy white coveralls. When they came they were big enough for men twice our size. Also there had been a slap-stick run-in with Lindbergh, later to be known as the "Lone Eagle" and a man who even then was a "loner."

It was a cadet tradition that, on the first pay day, the class held a dance at the St. Anthony Roof in San Antonio. Everybody kicked in five dollars except Lindbergh.

When he showed up at the dance we gave him the bum's rush.

I grinned to myself, too, as the car hummed steadily toward Chicago, about the visit I received from an old Galesburg friend who had hit it big in the oil business in Texas. His name was Dorcas Watson and he always had been a loud, brassy type.

He wasn't any different when he arrived at Kelly Field looking for me. As he drove his long, gleaming Pierce Arrow up to the gate, the officer of the day, wearing a dress sword, happened to be standing near the entrance.

"Hey, you, the boy with the knife," Watson bellowed. "Where'll I find a guy named Paul Robsky?"

It took me a long time to live that one down.

There was pain, too, in the memory of those days. Such as the afternoon when Jack Strickland, my drawling buddy from Alabama, spun in with his instructor. I sat beside his bed throughout the three nights before he died and after that everything seemed to go from bad to worse. I finally soloed but the acrobatics instructor didn't like the manner in which I did wingovers. Suffice it to say that in July of 1925 I washed out of the Air Corps. I had the consolation, however, of knowing that only twelve men graduated, including Lindbergh, in a class of one hundred and fifty.

Hanging around San Antonio, hating to go home as a failure, I took a short-term job repossessing automobiles for a finance company. At this point my spirits were revived by a letter from an old Air Force friend. There was a great deal of banditry in Mexico, he wrote, and he was flying payrolls in to isolated oil wells from Tampico. There was, he wrote, an opening if I was interested.

I was, but the job only lasted one hop. Celebrating with my first pay check in a Tampico cantina and being young and unattached, I picked up a slender, dark-haired Mexican girl with all of the proper female equipment. We were in a very intimate mood in her room when her "husband" showed up. It was the old badger game and I wasn't one to hold still for it. When I refused to pay off, he came at me with a large and ready knife. I crowned him quite decisively with a chair. I didn't like the limp manner in which he fell nor the racket the girl was making. She sure could scream. I hotfooted it to the harbor and fortunately obtained passage on an American tramp ship which was just pulling up anchor.

Arriving subsequently in New Orleans, I had been flat broke. This was solved, temporarily, by a job as time-keeper on a fruit company plantation but one month of that solitude was all I could take. Walking down the street in New Orleans that November of 1925 I saw a familiar face surmounting a new uniform. It was a friend of mine named Harold Jordan, who also had washed out of the Air Corps but had enlisted in the Marines and at this point was the recruiting officer in New Orleans.

"Why not join up?" he said over a schooner of beer and the free lunch which I was munching with gusto. "I've got forty recruits that are shipping out for Parris Island tomorrow morning and you can take charge of them for me."

So there I was, on my way to take boot training at Parris Island. Once there, I immediately put in for air duty and six weeks later I was shipped on to Quantico and assigned to a Vought Observation Squadron. My commanding officer was a lieutenant named Sandy Sanderson, who later made quite a name for himself as a general in the Pacific during World War II.

At Quantico I had received my rating as a gunnery sergeant. My duties consisted of photographic work in the morning and flying in the afternoon. And the photographic work was what, in the long run, put me in this car heading for Chicago right this moment. Because in April of 1926 I began to develop blisters on my hands from constant use of a too-powerful developing solution. I didn't think anything of it at first, treating it myself, but it was what eventually was to separate me from the service and lead me into the Prohibition Bureau.

Just at the time the trouble first started with my hands, my outfit was ordered to Nicaragua for active duty in one of those banana revolutions. But by the time the U.S.S. *Henderson* landed us there the blisters on my hands had become tremendously enlarged and were running copiously. Before I knew it, the medics ordered me sent back to Quantico and, after a couple of months in the base hospital, I was sent to the naval hospital in Washington.

I'll never forget my envy when, in May of 1927, while I was in the naval hospital, my former fellow air cadet, Lindbergh, made his history-making flight across the Atlantic. After reading the details, I flung the newspaper on the floor in disgust.

"Isn't that a fine way to act," snapped a passing nurse, picking up the paper and stacking the various sections neatly on my lap.

I just sat there, without a reply, and stared at the paper. Finally my eyes centered on a small item at the bottom of one of the pages. It said simply that there had been twenty thousand applicants for two thousand government jobs as Prohibition Bureau agents.

"Now there are some real odds," I commented to a fellow patient in the ward. "I think I'll apply to take the Civil Service examination when I get out of here next week just to see whether I can beat them."

Which is what I did after my eventual hospital release and service discharge. Not because I had anything personal against drinking. If I had any feelings along these lines, it was a moral certainty that no one had the right to tell somebody else not to drink. I always had consumed my share and enjoyed being with others who did, too. Yet, if anything came of this, I reasoned at the time, it sounded like it might be interesting and exciting.

So I took the examination and then headed for a convalescent visit on the large farm which my bachelor uncle, Ed Robsky, owned at Moseley, Virginia.

Uncle Ed was my favorite relative and was known to everybody in the vicinity as "Barefoot Ed" because of a penchant for walking around without shoes. Crowding seventy, he was a short, bald man with a pot belly and a walrus moustache. Generous to the point of fault, Uncle

Ed also was highly pugnacious. It was his boast that he could lick anybody, any time, and he had proved it on numerous occasions. He was proud of me as "the only one in the whole damned family with any gumption" and made me welcome on the promise that I "just sit and rest."

Uncle Ed grew a great deal of corn on his farm and its transformation into corn whiskey was something on which he prided himself. There was a wood-burning stove in the kitchen of the farmhouse and, instead of chairs, Uncle Ed simply installed a row of kegs filled with aging corn whiskey in a semicircle around the stove. That's where his visitors sat.

That's also where I was sitting one late November afternoon in 1928 when Ed Lacey, a neighbor who was a former Marine, too, came in obviously bearing news.

"Hey, Paul," he told me, "there's a government investigator been all over town asking about you. Seems like he wants to know about your reputation, what kind of a fellah you are and whether you ever been in trouble. You ain't been in trouble, have you?"

"Not that I know about," I said, completely forgetting the Civil Service examination I had taken and remembering only that incident in Tampico which, as far as I knew, might still be causing repercussions.

"Here he comes up the road now," Lacey said suddenly. "I'd know that green car anywhere."

The car continued on past the house and within a couple of days I had forgotten all about the incident. But then Uncle Ed brought me a letter. It was from the Prohibition Bureau, advising me that the Civil Service Commission had investigated and certified me to become an agent.

All while I was sitting on a keg of Uncle Ed's bootleg whiskey!

I was ordered to report in Richmond, Virginia, and, before I left, Uncle Ed tearfully wiped his eyes and wished me luck.

"But let me tell you one thing, boy," he said suddenly,

his chin jutting out. "You ever turn me in and I'll beat hell out of you."

"Well, now, Uncle Ed," I kidded him, "if I'm a Prohibition agent how can I keep from pulling you in."

"There's a lot of others around," he shot back. "Just you go take care of them and when you're all finished, why then you come get me."

After another interview in Richmond I was ordered to report to Greenville, South Carolina, on December 1, 1928. The following ten months had been everything I desired in the way of action and excitement.

How would it be in Chicago, I wondered now. Because the crouching Carolina mountains, with their smell of lichen and fern and the fragrance of the ever-present pines, had fastened an unyielding grip upon me. I would miss their grandeur and countless little things, such as the way in which smoke curled lazily from occasional cabins which nestled cautiously in the laurel like frightened rabbits.

Fast friendships had been the hardest to leave behind and already I felt a loneliness for the man who had taught me the ways of the mountains and their people. In my mind's eye I could picture massive Ed Austin and the manner in which his full, resonant voice rumbled up out of his deep chest while tiny laugh lines crinkled at the corners of his deep blue eyes.

It was Austin who had taken me under his wing and showed me the intricacies of being a "revenooer." I couldn't suppress a chuckle as I recalled the first of many humorous tricks he had played on me. It happened when I still was pea green to the business and Austin and I located a cache of twenty-five barrels hidden in the underbrush.

"Mr. Robsky," he had said like a lecturer in a classroom, "this here is something you have to learn."

With that he picked up an axe and with one quick expert swing cut the hoop at one end of the keg. He then repeated the process on the hoop at the other end, smashed in top and botton, and with one more good wallop on the stays completely demolished the barrel.

Stepping back and handing me the axe, he had instructed:

"Now, Mr. Robsky, let me see if you can do it."

My first attempt was a bungling one but Austin had cheered me on: "Not bad, Mr. Robsky. All you need is a little practice. If you keep at it, you'll get the hang of it."

I had been grimly determined to show him that I could do it as proficiently as he, so I concentrated doggedly on demolishing barrels. After working on about a dozen of them, I had finally gotten to the point where I could collapse one with a fair amount of dexterity. So I had called him over to where I was working.

"Mr. Austin, how's this?" I asked, proceeding to callapse one of the barrels with what I considered fair speed.

"Not bad, not bad," he nodded. "All you need is a bit more practice."

So, despite blisters which formed on my hands as I whacked my way through the metal hoops and protesting back muscles which ached from the unaccustomed exercise, I kept steadily at it until I had demolished every single barrel.

"Pretty good," Austin complimented from where he sat leaning against the trunk of a tree watching. "Just a bit more practice and damned if you won't be as good as I am."

And "practice" I got. For I had cut up every single barrel we found during the next few months before it suddenly came to me that I was doing all the work—while Austin sat watching me and delivering homespun philosophy anent my progress.

"Well now," he laughed when I finally mentioned it to him, "I was wondering when you were going to catch up to me, Mr. Robsky. And, you know, it took you a bit longer than I thought it would."

"All right," I had replied ruefully, "but maybe sooner or later I'll be able to teach you something."

Austin had cocked his head on one side, pushed his hat back from his eyes with one big thumb, and grunted:

"Mr. Robsky, just what do you think that might be?"

Quickly I had seen a fine opportunity to square accounts. For I had noticed, on one occasion when Austin had let fly a shot in hopes of frightening one fleeing moonshiner into halting, that he had held his revolver in both hands. This, I had discovered, was a trait peculiar to the mountain people. They almost all believed that any hand-held weapon had to be either clasped with both hands or steadied across the forearm of the idle hand, that is, shooting over the left forearm to steady the gun if you were right-handed.

Not too much earlier I had qualified as an expert pistol shot in the Marine Corps, shooting with the straight-arm or extended arm method.

"I'll tell you what I'll do," I said. "I'll bet you the next twenty-five barrels, loser to demolish them, that I can outshoot you on two shots at any target you pick."

Austin plucked at his lip, looked over to a steel drum used as a furnace in the still we had just raided and then pointed to it.

"All right, Mr. Robsky," he agreed. "That drum seems to be about 75 feet away. Two shots each at the bung hole. After you, Mr. Robsky."

Checking my .45 automatic, I took my stance and held my right arm extended to aim the pistol while bracing my left arm against my side. Austin watched me scornfully.

"Hell," he had growled, "you probably won't even hit the barrel holding the gun that way."

Lowering my pistol, I turned to him and said:

"Shall we make it fifty barrels, Mr. Austin?"

Nodding vigorously he chuckled: "You're on, Mr. Robsky."

With that, I took my stance again and the sound of the .45 reverberated through the mountain hollow.

"Missed the whole damned barrel," Austin crowed.

"I don't think so," I told him, and then squeezed off my second shot. We could see the metal fly up at the edge of the bung hole and, striding to the barrel, we saw where both bullets had emerged on the back side.

"It's pretty obvious," I had asserted, unable to repress

the satisfaction in my voice, "that the first shot went in the hole."

Austin grunted, walked back to the spot from which I had taken my shots, and held his pistol out in front of him with both hands. He was so shaken that his first shot missed the barrel completely. The second one hit the barrel about a foot from the hole.

Austin gulped and asked weakly: "How many barrels did we say, Mr. Robsky?"

"Fifty, Mr. Austin, exactly fifty," I had told him with malicious satisfaction as I looked down at my blistered hands.

And during the succeeding days I had lazed contentedly with my back to the trunk of a tree and watched complacently as Austin demolished our captured barrels, with me counting them off one by one all the way to fifty.

"That," I told him at last, "is number fifty, Mr. Austin. Would you mind, sir, if I gave you a hand from now on?"

Austin threw down the axe, sat down beside me with a hearty laugh and stuck out his massive hand.

"Mr. Robsky," he chuckled, "it seems I might have underestimated you. You'll do to take along."

It hadn't all been barrel breaking during those ten months, I remembered soberly. There had been a wild ride down a mountain at sixty miles an hour with me perched on top of a bootlegger's car before a crackup in which he was killed and I suffered a cracked ankle. There had been pitched battles by day and night as we were caught in the middle of a mountain feud and, on quite a few occasions, I felt I had been lucky to escape with my life.

I knew that Austin, too, had hated to see me leave when the summons came for me to report to Washington for a new assignment. It always had been his habit to call me "Mr. Robsky." When I left, big Ed stuck out one of those ham-like hands and his voice was gruff.

"So long, Mr. Robsky." Then he reached out and, gripping my shoulder, added quietly, "Take care of yourself, Paul. And if'n you don't like it there, c'mon back here."

So I had left the mountains behind me and, when I reached Washington, my instructions were brief and to the point.

"Here are the keys to a new car. Deliver it to Chicago and report to Assistant United States Attorney General William J. Froelich."

I had been nonplussed.

"What's this all about? Am I to be stationed in Chicago?"

"Search me," replied the agent in the Washington bureau. "That's all I know about it."

So I had taken the new car and set forth for Chicago. Not knowing what was ahead, I had occupied myself on the lonesome ride with memories of the past. But I'm not so sure, if I had known what I was heading into, that I might not have turned the car around and headed back to Greenville.

CHAPTER 2

It was late in the evening, much too late to report as ordered, when I finally arrived in Chicago. So I parked the car, found myself a hotel room and impatiently waited for morning, wondering, as I had been doing ever since leaving Washington, what this was all about.

I wasn't long learning the details when, early the next day, I found my way to the federal building and entered the office of Assistant United States Attorney General William J. Froelich.

The outer office was empty except for a woman behind the reception desk.

"Paul Robsky from the Prohibition Bureau in Washington," I told her. "I'm supposed to see Mister Froelich."

She nodded. "Take a seat and I'll tell him you're here."

I didn't even have time to sit down before the door to the inner office was thrown open and a tall man in his middle thirties came out briskly and offered me his hand.

"I'm Froelich," he said with a white-toothed smile. "Glad you got here all right. Come on inside."

I liked him on first sight, this man who was well-groomed and had a direct, easy manner of speaking. He motioned me to a chair and then, sliding into a swivel chair behind his desk, looked at me over tented fingers for several seconds.

"You kind of surprise me," he smiled, surveying my five feet, 10 inches and 170 pounds. "I kind of thought you'd be bigger."

"Well," I grinned back, "if you want somebody to

move pianos I'd just as soon you got yourself another boy."

Froelich chuckled. "No, not pianos. But it might be even more difficult than that. No offense meant, Mister Robsky. I've read your record and I'm sure you'll do. Your references are damned good and that's why you were picked for this assignment."

"Must be something big," I suggested. "They couldn't even give me a hint in Washington."

He nodded.

"It's big all right and, until we get settled and into operation, it's on the secret side, too."

"Well," I asked, "is it too early to tell me what it's all about?"

He tented his fingers again and a grim note entered his voice as he began to speak.

"You've heard of Al Capone? Well, we're going to run him right out of business."

My eyebrows shot up but he waved me to silence and continued.

"I've been sent here from Washington for the express purpose of coordinating the forces which we believe will get that job done. We are forming two units which will operate independently: completely independent of all bureau ties and accountable to no one but me.

"One unit is from the treasury department," he continued. "It will be their job to gather and correlate information on Capone's various forms of income. There isn't much question but what he has been failing to pay a tremendous amount of income taxes and we feel that this may be the best manner in which to obtain a conviction which would remove him from circulation."

Froelich's voice flowed on as I sat forward in my chair and listened intently.

"The other unit is being composed of hand-picked agents from the Prohibition Bureau. We know that a great many prohibition men haven't been doing the job for which they are being paid. Undoubtedly the principal reason is because they are being paid a great deal more by

outside sources, such as the Capone mob, to look the
other way. We have scanned the lists for men whose
records show that they have been incorruptible and
fearless. We are going to dry up Capone so that he no
longer can pay for 'protection' and we feel certain that in
so doing we will flush the rats out of their holes."

"It'll probably take some doing," I suggested as he
paused.

Again he nodded.

"Yes, it's a highly dangerous assignment. They won't
take it lying down, you can be certain of that. But remember this, we won't take anything lying down, either. We'll
answer threats with action and violence with violence.

"These orders," he said, "come straight from the White
House."

"That's good enough for me," I told him flatly.

"Good," Froelich smiled. "Glad to have you aboard."

The interoffice phone buzzed and Froelich picked it up
and I heard him say "Send them in."

"Nice that you arrived now," he said as he cradled the
receiver on its hook. "I had an organizational meeting set
up for this morning with the men with whom you will
work. They're here now. Maybe you know some of
them."

But, as eight men filed into the office and Froelich
stood up to make introductions, I saw that they were all
strangers to me.

"Gentlemen," he began, "this is Paul Robsky from the
Greenville office. He's joining us in our little enterprise."

One by one they stepped forward and shook hands. I
had the feeling that each one of them was placing me under a microscope. I was looking them over, too.

"Eliot Ness," said Froelich. "He'll be my chief liaison
man." He was boyish looking with an open, innocent face
and, I judged, about my size. Ness appeared the quiet
type, albeit capable.

"Glad you're here," he said in a low voice.

Froelich motioned to the next man and said "Joe
Leeson." And this was all man, six feet, two inches tall,

rock-hard from the look of him, with a jutting chin and granite-hard eyes. His massive hand smothered mine in a hard, horny grip. He bobbed his head and moved away with cat-like grace.

"Nice to meet you," pleasantly said the third, a tall, lean, scholarly looking man who was tastefully dressed. "I'm Lyle Chapman."

The fourth was big, too. His face was the map of Ireland and his blue eyes smiled as we shook hands. "Marty Lahart," he grinned. I couldn't help but smile back.

I began to feel like a midget as the fifth one approached and held out a ham-like hand. Six feet two and about 220 pounds, his face was expressionless and his eyes bored into me like a gimlet. The voice was flat as he grunted "Sam Seager."

Another behemoth loomed behind him, bulky and with a walrus moustache. "Me, I'm George Steelman. Good to see you."

The two who remained were more my size. "I'm Jim Taylor," said the slim one with what seemed to be a perpetual frown etched on his forehead. "And me," concluded the last of the group, a rangy, dapper man with a pencil-line moustache, "I'm Arnold Grant."

I was to get to know all of them better, much better, in the days ahead but now we took seats in chairs arranged in a semicircle around Froelich's desk.

The Assistant United States Attorney General didn't waste any time.

"I think we're about ready to go to work," he said. "I've arranged offices for you men in the Transportation Building. You all will be on a per diem. In your reports to Washington simply make them read 'Special assignment, Chicago.' You'll have no hours and I'll back you up to the limit; any limit. The important thing is results.

"What we want," he went on without pause, "is to dry up Chicago. I mean bone dry. I want every brewery and every still found and destroyed. Any records you get in the process will be invaluable. I'll turn them over to the treasury unit for processing. They'll handle the paper work. But from you men I want concrete action."

We all nodded and Froelich continued minus interruption.

"I've given a great deal of thought to how you might start operating, although you men all have fine reputations as crackerjacks in finding illicit liquor and the people who make it and distribute it. If you don't mind the suggestion, I have the feeling that you'd work better in two-man teams, pooling our manpower only when we have something real hot to handle. That way we can really blanket this town. As I said, Ness will be my liaison man and we'll split the remainder of you up in pairs."

This we proceeded to do and I drew Steelman, the big man with the walrus moustache, as my sidekick. I figured I was lucky. For, while we were pairing up, I had learned that he had been selected for the squad from the Chicago bureau and, while I was from Galesburg, in Illinois, I never had made more than an occasional visit to the city and was glad to have been paired with someone who knew it so well geographically.

As the meeting broke up, I approached Froelich's desk and said that I'd like to have a receipt for the new car I had delivered.

"Sure," he said, giving me the receipt. Then he tossed the keys back to me. "You'll have to have a car. Use this one as long as this assignment lasts."

That easily I had a partner and a car, but I still didn't have a place to live. And in the next several days, as I hunted for an apartment in company with my new partner, Steelman, I not only learned much about him but also the fact that he apparently didn't feel we would be able to make much of a dent in the Capone empire. I could appreciate his sentiments somewhat as I began to assimilate the feeling in Chicago toward the underworld chieftain.

The basic ingredient, of course, was fear of underworld retribution against anyone who did anything against him or his underlings. But it extended far beyond that. There is always somebody on the "take" wherever there is easy money and yet, in the South where I had worked, enforcement was basically clean as far as prohibition agents were concerned.

In Chicago it seemed that everyone was against us. Steelman made no bones of the fact that most of the agents in the Chicago bureau had their hands out.

"The police in this town, or about ninety per cent of them, are rotten with easy money," he told me. "The people on the whole naturally support the setup because if nobody drank, what would be the use of making all this beer and liquor? It's a lousy mess and you can't hardly blame some of the guys for taking dough."

I felt him staring at me as he said it, a peculiar, searching inspection.

"Well, don't look at me," I said. "Understand, I've got nothing against drinking. As a matter of fact, I drink my share when I can get it. But as long as we're being paid to do this job, by God I'm gonna try to do it."

I thought it was an exceptionally long while before he said, "Me, too."

But I got the idea of what he had been talking about driven home to me when I found an apartment that I liked and told the superintendent that I'd take it. He produced a form to fill out, one of the questions on it asking for the tenant's occupation.

"Prohibition agent?" he frowned when I had filled it out and handed it to him. "I'm sorry, Mister Robsky, but I just remembered this apartment has an option taken on it."

"Bullshit," Steelman snorted.

"Okay," the super said shortly. "We just don't want you kind of guys around here. It ain't healthy and—what t'hell, we just don't want you."

"I guess you can't hardly blame them," Steelman shrugged when we were outside again. "Y'know, I been in this town a long time and, let's face it, Capone has bought a lot of loyalty. Let us pick up one of his guys, let's say just an ordinary truck driver who makes fifty to sixty bucks a week, and the guy is defended in court for free. If he goes to the can, his family receives his salary all the time he's in the jug. It's a hard system to beat."

How hard I realized some time later after I did manage to rent a small, comfortable apartment and became friendly with a shapely, pretty girl who lived next door to me. This budding friendship was nipped in the bud when she found out what I did.

"Let me tell you something," she said as we had our first—and last—dinner date. "I been married and I got a kid. Well, my husband took a powder and I was in a real jam. I had a girl friend who worked in a night spot and she told me to go see Al Capone."

Desperate, she had gone to see the scarfaced man with an introduction from her friend. Capone, she said, had been polite and kindly.

"One of the goons working for him patted me on the fanny as I started to leave and said that anybody as pretty as I was shouldn't have to work," she said. "He told me in no uncertain terms that he'd be glad to take care of me. Capone happened to overhear his remarks. He came out from behind his desk and slapped this goon across the face and told him to keep his mouth shut and his hands to himself. About a week later I got a call from a night spot and I'm still working there as a hat-check girl.

"So," she said, getting up and grabbing her wrap, "you know what I think of Al Capone—and thanks for the meal."

That was the last date I ever had with her, though, to be frank, I tried several times later. It simply seemed as if the whole city of Chicago was against anybody who had any designs on Capone.

Except, it might be added, for a dissatisfied few.

Like the night when we were first getting our feet on the ground and Steelman and I were having a midnight snack at a greasy-spoon lunch counter on the South Side after cruising the neighborhood without being able to detect anything suspicious.

George was talking to a chance acquaintance and I had

gone outside for a breath of air when a prowl car drew up to the curb and two policemen got out. One went into the restaurant and the other, a sergeant, walked over to me.

"Hey," he said, "ain't you one of this new hot-shot group of prohibition guys who are supposed to be so damned honest?"

"Yeah," I replied, "but how do you know so much about it?"

"Never mind," he said. "We know what goes on around here."

Surreptitiously he looked around and then, seeing no one else, lowered his voice and said confidentially: "I'm gonna do you a favor. I'm gonna tell you where there's a drop, a spot where they leave the stuff for local delivery."

I was more curious than anything else at this volunteered information.

"How come you know so much about it and haven't done anything?"

"Hell," he barked, looking around again to be certain that no one else was listening. "I'll be frank with you and call you a liar if you say I said this. But those dirty bastards are only giving me twenty-five bucks a month. I told 'em I wanted more and they just laughed at me. Maybe now they'll laugh on the other side of their face. And I'll tell you something else. If they don't come through after this I'll give you some more spots."

Steelman appeared in the restaurant doorway about this time and the sergeant whispered an address and, brushing past Steelman, walked into the restaurant.

"Come on," I told Steelman. "I think I've got something."

"What is it?" he asked intently.

"I've got an address of a drop," I told him. "Let's go see what's doing there."

Steelman was unexpectedly reluctant.

"Maybe we ought to get the rest of the squad, stake it out and watch it a while before we do anything."

I was impatient and wouldn't be denied.

"Hell's fire," I burst out, "just lead me to this address and stop all the nonsense."

Steelman grumbled some more but at my continued insistence directed me to the address the sergeant had given me, which turned out to be a garage in an alley. I parked a few doors away and we approached it on foot.

They certainly weren't afraid of interference. The doors to the garage stood wide open. Inside was a large truck and three men were icing down five hundred barrels of beer with huge cakes of ice. Stopping what they were doing, the men watched us approach and, when we were a few feet away, I told them:

"We're federal officers. You guys are under arrest."

One of them bolted past us and out the door. The two others tried to make it out a side door but I laid out one of them with the barrel of my .45 and the other meekly held up his hands.

"Keep 'em covered," I yelled at Steelman, and took out the door after the other one.

He was a half block away and, as I set out after him, a prowl car came along.

"Catch that guy," I shouted. "He just pulled a stickup."

They caught him at the next corner and when I got there I told them I'd take over.

"This is our pinch," one policeman argued.

"I'm a federal man," I said. "This guy is a bootlegger."

The cop was so mad he turned red.

"What the hell's the idea of telling us he was a stickup guy if he's only a bootlegger? You got a lot of guts."

I was getting mad, too.

"What do you mean, 'only' a bootlegger? Don't you guys get paid for catching bootleggers, too, or are you paid not to?"

I thought he was going to swing at me, but he said a few nasty things about prohibition agents, jumped back in the prowl car and sped off. Then I escorted my prisoner back to the garage and Steelman and I took the three of them to the local precinct house and booked them.

I had made a mental note of the shield number of the sergeant who had given me the tip so it was an easy matter to obtain his name and home address. About a week later, when I hadn't heard any more from him, I went to his home and he answered the door.

"Thanks for the tip," I told him. "Got anything else?"

"Nope, and thank you," he grinned. "The mob came through with more money when they found out I meant business. So you and I have nothing more to discuss."

With that he went inside and slammed the door in my face. I wanted to beat hell out of him but I figured finally that it would be a waste of time.

Shortly after this, Steelman and I were called into Froelich's office and advised that the whole squad was being gathered that night for a raid on a Lumber Street brewery which had been uncovered by Leeson and Chapman.

We gathered at about ten o'clock that night and made our way to the vicinity in two cars. Leeson and Chapman, who knew the layout, directed their own project. We surrounded the place with Leeson leading one group in through the double front doors and Steelman and I in the detail assigned to crash in the back. On a prearranged signal, we started battering down the doors, our axes and crowbars making a terrific racket.

It was a fiasco.

When we hammered down the doors and got inside there wasn't a truck or a piece of apparatus in the place. There was plenty of evidence that this had, indeed, been a big operation. But now there wasn't anything except one lonely rat as big as a cat which scuttled across the floor and disappeared into a hole in one corner of the echoing room.

Leeson was in a rage.

"I'll be damned," he stormed. "This place was swinging last night. Now look. Not a damned bottle cap."

"I don't understand it," the frowning Chapman said quietly. "I know we had this pegged. How do you suppose they got wind that we were going to call?"

"I wonder," Leeson growled, glaring at us individually.

At the time, I didn't think any more about it. Instead, Steelman and I devoted our efforts the next few days to following trucks from a barrel-washing plant. The trail led to a "cooling off" garage where, we supposed, the barrels were held before they could be moved to a brewery. We didn't suspect that it was a drop.

"Hell," Steelman said after we had sat there for several days without any trucks reappearing, "we must have a bum steer here. Let's chuck it. Besides, I wanta knock off and see a guy in the next block."

The thought came to me that possibly there was another exit in the rear. I didn't mention it to Steelman but thought I'd just check it out myself.

"Okay," I said. "I'll see you later."

My timing couldn't have been more perfect. Because just as I circled the block and drove around to the rear of the garage, a black sedan pulled out followed by a van whose canvas covering couldn't disguise the barrels underneath. Cautiously I tailed them on a winding journey through the South Side. I was completely lost when the truck halted finally and the driver began to unload barrels of beer at what was undoubtedly a speakeasy.

Leaving my car parked a half block behind the truck, I made my way up to where the driver was unloading. He didn't notice me until I was right on him.

"Get 'em up," I snapped, holding my pistol on him. "I'm a federal agent. Just put your hands against the wall and take it easy."

A quick search showed him to be unarmed and I snapped on the handcuffs, boosted him into the cab of the truck and started driving it back uptown. I was congratulating myself on the ease with which I had accomplished this arrest but I had forgotten one thing. That was the lead car.

For I had gone only about a block, unconsciously passing the lead car, when it pulled up beside me and tried to cut me off. There was a grinding of metal as I rode him off and a nervous sweat broke out on my forehead. The handcuffed driver was sweating, too.

"Lissen, why don't you be smart and play ball?" he sputtered. "There's plenty of money in it for you. But my boss is hard to get along with and he ain't gonna like this at all."

Now the car was alongside me again and, a quick look disclosed, the driver was leaning over toward the right window with a gun in his hand. Just then he let go with a shot that spanged against the metal roof of the cab and the guy beside me yelled: "That Malone is gonna kill both of us."

My nervousness had given way to anger now and, as he loosed another shot, I spun the wheel and there was the scream of metal as the truck pinned the car to the wall of the alley. Both truck and car crunched to a jolting stop and the man beside me was thrown against the windshield and knocked cold.

A tight grip on the wheel had saved me. Clambering across my unconscious prisoner, I threw open the right-hand door and leaped out. With my .45 in my fist, I ran around the back of the truck. The car, a black sedan, had jammed into the wall and steam was hissing from its battered radiator. The truck had skidded along its side and both doors had been torn off.

"All right," I panted, "come out of there or I'm going to cut loose."

There wasn't a sound. Inching forward, I looked inside and saw that the driver of the car had been knocked unconscious. I reached in and hauled him out by the collar and as I did so, his pistol clattered to the alley cobblestones beside him. Just as I reached down and stuffed it into the waistband of my trousers, he began to stir.

"Okay," I told him roughly, "on your feet and no more nonsense."

He was a burly, broad-shouldered man with bristling sandy hair and fierce, red-rimmed eyes. There wasn't a word out of him until I had him back in the cab of the truck, handcuffed to my other prisoner. Then his eyes centered on me and his voice grated against my ears.

"You are going to be paid off for this, but real good."

"I told you he wouldn't like it," the driver yelped. "Red Malone don't . . ."

"Shut up," the big man interrupted him coldly.

The driver swallowed hard and clamped his lips together. We drove in silence until, finally, I found my way back downtown to the Transportation Building. Then, leaving the truck in a no-parking zone, I herded the two of them upstairs.

Big Joe Leeson was alone in the office, holding down liaison duties for the day.

"Steelman called in and checked off for the day," he said. "He said he didn't know where you had gone. I was beginning to wonder what happened to you. I was even starting to worry a little."

Sneeringly, the ugly Malone broke in.

"You can keep right on worryin' because I ain't done with this nosey bastard yet."

The iron-hard Leeson, as I was to learn much better at a later date, was a pugnacious man who hated hoods. Now his voice was suspiciously soft.

"Take the cuffs off this guy," he ordered me.

I did.

"Okay, tough guy," Leeson barked, shoving his big chin into Malone's evil face, "suppose you start with me. And here's something to give you an excuse."

With that, Leeson hauled off and knocked the guy flat before I knew what was on his mind. Malone made no effort to get up, simply staring at Leeson with narrowed eyes.

"You'll get yours, too," he glowered.

"Well, there's no time like right now, big mouth," Leeson told him. "Get up, if you've got the guts."

Malone sat still, rubbing a trickle of blood from his lip with the back of one hairy hand. He wanted no more of Leeson.

We booked them then and, as we returned to the office

Leeson asked me, "Where's the speakeasy where they were delivering?"

I stopped dead, feeling foolish.

"Damned if I know. I don't know much about Chicago and they plumb lost me driving 'round and 'round before I made the pinch. As a matter of fact, I don't even know where I left my own car."

So, with the laughing Leeson, I spent the rest of the day "driving 'round and 'round" some more through the South Side until I finally located the wrecked sedan.

That night we raided the speak and closed it up, too.

But I realized a short time later how close a call I had when Malone was taking pot shots at me with his pistol. Shortly after getting out on bail, he got mad at his wife and cut her throat. Then to make the job complete, he used the same knife to kill their pet police dog. After that, Malone, who was a psycho much feared even in Chicago's deadly underworld, simply vanished and, as far as I know, hasn't been caught yet.

When I saw the story of the slaying in the newspapers, I called it to Leeson's attention on a visit to the office.

"I guess I was lucky again."

"What do you mean, 'again'?" he demanded.

"Well," I related, "down in Greenville I worked with a fellow named Austin and one day he started up one side of a mountain and told me to go around the other side and meet him from the other direction. Like this time, I got lost and came upon a ramshackle old cabin. All of a sudden there's a raggedy old guy with a long beard holding a squirrel rifle on me kind of nonchalant like."

"Go on," Leeson grinned as I stopped for breath.

"Well, I asked him if he could tell me how to find the main road and he says to me 'Be yo' new 'roun chere, young'n?' I told him I sure was and he asked me 'Be yo' with Austin?' I said I was and he told me to turn around and follow a long-disused wagon trail to the main road.

"I did," I continued, "and finally I found, or was found, by Austin, an old hand in the mountains. Austin lost a little of his color when I told him what happened.

" 'By God, Mr. Robsky,' he told me, 'you sure are a lucky man. That was old man Plumber. He was serving eight to ten years for murder down in the penitentiary in Columbia when he got away and they been tryin' to catch him for a helluva while. He's dangerous as hell. The only thing I can figure is that old Plumber thought you was just a babe in the woods, decided you were too dumb to kill and just let you live."

Leeson laughed and sobered.

"You were double damned lucky this time," he said. "That Malone would have killed you dead just for practice."

I knew he wasn't kidding, either.

CHAPTER 3

It wasn't long after the incident with Malone that I had to admit to myself that I still must be the babe-in-the-woods that old Plumber considered me to be back there in the mountains of South Carolina.

Locating the breweries, almost from the first, wasn't easy. The mob even in the beginning seemed to know almost as much about us and our plans as we did. The "protection" they paid had given them a fairly free hand until our arrival on the scene and now they began to take extra precautions.

These maneuvers included the use of barrels of moth balls to overpower the usual brewery smells. Doors and windows also were blacked out with black paint, cloth coverings or other padding. They also began to convoy their larger and more valuable loads with a carload of hoods up front and another trailing behind.

There were only two alternatives. One was the laborious, time-consuming method of back-tracking barrels picked up at a speakeasy. This meant tracing them back to the washing plant, to the cooling off spot where they were held until the mobsters felt they were free of surveillance and, finally, to the brewery. If we were observed at any one stage of the process all we wound up with was a load of empty barrels.

The other method was simply to go on an all-night prowl and try to blunder onto something.

One night I was driving slowly through the South Side with Steelman, who seemed even more morose than usual, when I spotted a warehouse on South Street which looked

37

like a perfect spot to me. A vacant lot, overgrown with high weeds, stretched from the warehouse to the next corner.

"Let's check that one out," I said to George as I wheeled around the corner, parked and cut the lights. I opened the car door and got out.

"I'll take a look over there and see if there's anything stirring."

"You're wasting your time." His voice followed me into the darkness.

I plunged into the weeds and had only gone a few feet when I heard a rustling all around me. Something brushed against my leg and I stopped and listened. The rustling continued, broken by a low incessant squeaking. Taking a pencil flashlight from my inside coat pocket I cut its beam toward the ground and beady little eyes gleamed up at me.

Rats! The field was alive with them.

I couldn't repress a shiver as I turned off the light. Then, locking my teeth, I headed again toward the building. Several more times the startled rats brushed my legs and I was in a cold sweat when I broke cautiously into the clear alongside the warehouse.

Carefully I made my way along to the back and there, opening onto an alley littered with trash, I found two wide doors. It was a perfect setup for a brewery. And, to make me even more suspicious, I saw with a quick flick of the pencil light that a little window in a small door beside the truck entrance had been painted black on the inside. However, there were no sounds from inside, no odor that I could detect and no obvious new tire tracks to be seen in another quick flick of the light.

But I couldn't still the hunch that this actually was a brewery.

Going to the corner of the building, I grubbed out a handful of dirt and scattered it loosely across the entranceway. It wouldn't be particularly noticeable to anyone but a later check would reveal tire tracks if there was any movement through those big double doors. Then I worked a match stick into the crack of the small door at about knee height. If anybody went in or out of this "empty" warehouse that way they would have to dislodge the match stick.

Satisfied that I could do no more at this time, I took a deep breath and plunged back through that rat-infested lot.

"Did you find anything?" Steelman asked as I approached the car. I wondered at the curiosity evident in his voice but dismissed it as interest in the job at hand.

"No, not a damned thing. All I saw was rats. God, there must be thousands of them in that field. I'd sooner walk through a pit full of snakes."

"I told you it was a waste of time," Steelman grumbled, slouching down in the seat beside me.

I was just telling him about the dirt and the match stick routines I had devised when a prowl car slid up alongside us and a beam of light shot into our faces.

"Hold it right there," said a voice from behind the light. "And don't try any tricks because you're covered."

"We're federal men," Steelman said as he sat upright.

"Never mind the baloney," the voice snapped back. "Just stay put."

The door on the other side of the prowl car slammed shut and swiftly a second cop appeared on my side of the car, a pistol ready in his hand.

"Out," he ordered.

"Listen," I protested, "we're prohibition agents. We just stopped here for a smoke." Knowing the reputation of the Chicago police, I wasn't about to tip our hand.

"Out," he repeated, gesturing with the pistol.

Slowly, so as not to give either one of them an excuse to start blasting, Steelman and I eased out of the car. I fumed as they relieved us of our pistols and then, taking their own sweet time, directed us to produce our identification.

"Well, well," nastily said one, a sergeant, "it looks like they're legitimate, or as legit as a prohibition agent can be."

I'd had about enough. "Put up that gun and I'll show you just how legitimate I am."

"Never mind showing us your muscles," he replied, handing back our pistols and identification. "But stay the hell out of our precinct. You guys are trying to make us look bad and every time I see any of you around I'm gonna roust you."

"It probably wouldn't be too tough to make you look bad," I told him, still boiling and ready to start swinging if that was the way they wanted it.

"Ah, the hell with 'em," Steelman intervened. "Let's get outta here."

Reluctantly, I got into the car and drove off with an angry grinding of gears.

"I told you it was a waste of time to begin with," Steelman commented acidly.

I was still mad the next morning and went down to Froelich's office with a chip on my shoulder. He listened with narrowed eyes as I told him what had happened.

"Any suggestions?" he asked when I finished.

"Yes, get us city detective badges. Then all we'll have to do is flash them and tell the uniformed cops to get lost."

The Assistant United States Attorney General nodded. "Can you come back in about an hour?"

"Sure," I said. And, when I returned an hour later, there were enough gold badges for every man in the squad on his desk.

"Take one for you and one for Steelman," Froelich said. "You're now detective lieutenants in the Chicago Police Department and you'll be backed up as such if necessary."

I was still burning. So that night I deliberately drove back into the same precinct, parking several blocks from the warehouse in which I was interested because I didn't want to reveal the fact that we were casing that one particular spot. As I suspected, within a short time the same prowl car pulled up beside us and again we were bathed in that strong beam of light.

"Hold it right there," the voice of the previous night said.

"You hold it," I cracked, holding up the detective lieutenant's badge so it gleamed in the light. "Now, put out that damned light."

The light snapped off and, getting out of the car, I stepped up to the prowl car and shoved the badge under the cop's nose. At the same time I threw the tiny beam of my pencil flashlight on the badge.

"Can you read what it says?" I snapped.

"Yes lieutenant," the policeman said in a subdued tone. "But . . ."

"Well, then, you smart bastards remember that things aren't always what they seem," I chewed him out. "Did you numbskulls ever think that maybe we were posing as feds?"

"We never thought . . ." he stuttered.

I shut him off quickly. "That's why you're still wearing a uniform, because you never think. Now, get the hell out of here and stay off our backs or you'll wish you had."

The prowl car took off with a roar and I wore a wide grin as I got back into the car.

"Now," I said to Steelman, "let's go case that South Street warehouse again."

"What for?" he protested. "I told you it's a waste of time. There isn't a damned thing there."

I was stubborn.

"I've just got to take a look even though it means walking through those rats again," I told him adamantly as I parked on the side street we had used before because it was out of sight of the warehouse. "You can wait if you want to."

Again Steelman sat in the car as I gritted my teeth and made my way through those rustling weeds. Then, when I arrived at the back of the warehouse, I checked the dirt I had strewn across the entrance and saw to my disappointment that there were no tire tracks. But my spirits lifted when I checked the small door and found that the match stick I had wedged in the crack was gone.

"Somebody was in there since last night," I reported to Steelman when I got back to the car. "The match I wedged in the door was gone."

He was unconvinced.

"You're nuts. It could have been the wind, or maybe even a bird."

I had to admit it was a possibility. But this time, I explained to him, I had put two matches between the door and the casing, jamming them in so tightly that only by the door being opened could they possibly be dislodged.

"I'm telling you again that you're wasting your time," he said almost angrily. "Let's get out of here."

He protested even more violently the next night when I again insisted on returning but again I ignored his objections.

This time I returned to the car in triumph.

"Not only were the matches gone," I crowed, "but there were several sets of tire tracks. I'm dead certain we've hit one."

Steelman was silent in the darkness. It was several minutes before he spoke.

"Maybe you're right," he admitted grudgingly. "But we'd better keep it under surveillance a couple more days and make certain before we get the whole gang down here and look like a bunch of chumps."

It sounded sensible enough to me and when, two nights later, we saw a heavily loaded truck rumble out of the warehouse, I told him I was going to set up the raid.

The next morning, as I walked into the lobby of the federal building on my way to see Froelich and set up the raid, I almost collided with a familiar thin-faced little man hurrying off the elevator. He made as if to turn away but I called to him and, as he hesitated, grabbed him by the elbow.

"O'Hara," I said. "Jim O'Hara. What the hell are you doing here in Chicago?"

O'Hara was an agent who had been stationed in Norfolk and whom I had met once in Greenville when he was there on some special assignment. I had been new to the service at the time and his reputation as a top-flight agent had made a lasting impression on me.

"Oh, hi," he said with what seemed at the moment to be almost reluctance. I assumed that he had forgotten my name and was somewhat embarrassed.

"Robsky, Paul Robsky," I said, holding out a hand which he shook perfunctorily. "I met you about a year or so ago in Greenville."

"Oh, sure," he nodded.

"What brings you here?" I asked. "You been transferred?"

His reply was terse.

"No, I just had to see about a few things. As a matter of fact I hate this town. Wouldn't work here. Gotta hurry now. See you later."

With that he spun on his heel and walked out. I stared after him for a moment, almost dumfounded at his tight-lipped dismissive manner and abrupt departure. Then I shrugged it off and almost immediately forgot about O'Hara as I took the elevator and walked into Froelich's office to set up my raid.

Froelich listened intently to my story of how we had located the South Street warehouse, making little comment, and nodded his agreement when I proposed that we hit it that very night. He said that he would notify the others and that we would all gather at the Transportation Building office at ten o'clock that evening.

The day seemed to crawl past as I waited impatiently for the time we would all meet. This was the first one I had located all by myself and I was certain that it would be a big one. Finally, however, the time arrived and the whole squad set out in two cars.

This was my baby and I had laid it out so that Steelman and I, along with Leeson and the scholarly Chapman would hit the truck entrance on the alley. The remainder were to break in from the front street entrance.

I felt more than the usual amount of excitement; my hopes were so high that I had hit on a big one. And it seemed to me that some of the others, notably Leeson,

Chapman and Ness, displayed a noticeable lack of enthusiasm. I remembered the way we all had been keyed up the night we hit the brewery found by Leeson and Chapman—the one that turned up empty. Maybe they thought this was another dud, I conjectured.

We had timed the raid for 11:30 p.m. and we drew up with a simultaneous rush at front and back. Leaping from the car, I shattered the glass window in the small door with my pistol, reached inside, fumbled for a few seconds for a bolt, found it and flung open the door. Leeson was right behind me as we swarmed inside, saw in the beam of our flashlights a crossbar on the wide garage doors and swiftly opened them to let in Steelman and Chapman.

In the darkness behind us I could hear a hollow reverberation as the others battered in the street door at the other end. Then the warehouse was flooded with light as Leeson found a switch and snapped it on. I stood there in wide-eyed disbelief, refusing to believe my eyes.

Empty!

The whole warehouse was absolutely naked, the only thing in sight being a rope ladder dangling from a loft. Chagrin flooded through me as I swarmed up the ladder and saw more of the same—absolutely nothing. I felt like a treed coon as I looked down at the silent circle of faces staring up at me from below.

Leeson's voice, biting and filled with sarcasm, boomed up at me. "Not a damned thing."

"Too late again," Chapmen commented. "But you can tell by the smell that they've been operating here."

Slowly I clambered down the rope ladder and we all filed out without talking, the only sound the scraping of our feet on the concrete floor. Nobody even spoke when I dropped off Leeson and Chapman. Only the usually morose and gruff Steelman was sympathetic.

Not a bad guy at that, I reasoned as he walked into his apartment and I drove away. At least he had been nice enough not to say "I told you so."

I was still at home the next afternoon when the telephone rang and Froelich's voice scratched its way over the wire.

"Paul?"

"Yeah."

"Can you drop down this afternoon? I'd like to talk to you."

"All right." Then, as an afterthought I added, "Anything special?"

"No. I just want to talk to you."

"Okay."

Probably wanted to chew me out about last night, I thought. Well, I could hardly blame him. I'd taken everybody on a wild goose chase and all I'd come up with was a dry hole.

Later in the day, as I walked into the federal building, I felt like a man marching out to face a firing squad. And as I went through the lobby toward the elevators, damned if I didn't bump into Jim O'Hara again. The hell with him, too, I thought, and started to walk on past.

"Hey, Paul," he said. "I'm leaving town in a few minutes. Glad I saw you."

He stuck out a hand, shook warmly and then waved and walked away with a parting smile.

"Well, I'll be damned," I looked after him in some amazement. "Now what the hell got into that guy to make him change about so suddenly."

Shrugging it off, I went on up to Froelich's office and the receptionist told me: "Go right on in. Mister Froelich's waiting for you."

Froelich greeted me warmly as I entered, got up and shook hands and motioned me to a chair.

"I thought I'd be persona non grata around here," I grinned wanly.

"Forget it," he said, his voice tightening. "You were sold out!"

I jerked erect in my chair.

"I was what?"

"You were sold out," he repeated. "So was Leeson on his raid."

I was stunned. All I could say, rather weakly, was "You're kidding."

"I wish I was but we've got the whole story," Froelich asserted.

"Who?"

Froelich leaned back in his chair with a tired sigh.

"Steelman."

At first I could hardly bring myself to believe it.

"Now wait a minute," I protested. "Steelman's been with me every night. Look, Bill, maybe it was those cops who tried to roust us when we were checking out that warehouse."

"No good," Froelich waved. "That's why I called you down here. To explain—and to apologize."

"Apologize?"

"Yes, we thought for a time that you were in it with him."

Now I was really stunned.

"Let me explain," Froelich said. "You may not have heard about it, but we've had a wire tap for some time on the Wabash Hotel where Guzik has his headquarters."

I didn't need him to tell me that Jake (Greasy Thumb) Guzik was the syndicate's treasurer. He, along with Ralph Capone and Frank (The Enforcer) Nitti, were the big guns while Scarface Al was serving out his year in Philadelphia on the firearms charge.

"Guzik handles the purse strings," Froelich went on. "So we knew that any large or unusual payoffs would have to be handled through him."

I sat quietly listening.

"Well, a few weeks back, shortly before the Leeson hit which turned up a dry hole on Lumber Street, one of the mob called Guzik and told him he had somebody who wanted to sell him some hot information. He told Guzik that the informer wanted five thousand dollars and said 'the guy swears it'll save us a hundred grand.' Guzik told him all right but that the guy had better produce—or else.

"As we found out later," Froelich told me, "it was Steelman selling us out on the Lumber Street job. This came out about a week ago—and Steelman made his big mistake—when he called Guzik directly."

The conversation, Froelich said, had gone like this:

"This is the G-man who put you wise to the Lumber Street raid."

"Yeah?"

"Well, I got something else. Me and my partner have found the big one on South Street. We'll lay off for a few days until you can clean it out but we want another five grand."

"Gangsters," Guzik ranted. "Five thousand is a lot of money. Make it two thousand."

"Nothing doing," Steelman replied. "We want five grand or else we'll knock it off right now."

Guzik finally agreed, Froelich said.

"But Steelman had kept using the word 'we' and naturally we all thought you were in on it," Froelich explained. "So we brought in an outside torpedo to check up on both of you."

A "torpedo" in the lingo of the Prohibition Bureau was an unknown operator from another section who was brought in to tail and check up on agents who were thought to have gone wrong.

Suddenly it dawned on me—O'Hara.

"Yeah, Jim O'Hara from Norfolk," I told Froelich.

His eyes widened.

"How did you know?"

"I didn't," I said, "I just this minute put two and two together. I saw him yesterday and he acted like I was poison. I just saw him a little while ago and he was right friendly. What a difference a day makes."

Froelich wore a broad smile.

"Yes, it wasn't until this morning that we really cleared you. I can tell you," he said, referring to some papers on his desk, "that you have thirty-five dollars and twenty cents in your bank account. Steelman, on the other hand, shortly after the Lumber Street raid, deposited five thousand dollars in his account.

"But what really cleared you was a call Steelman made

to the Wabash Hotel early this morning," he revealed. "It seems that something went wrong with the payoff on last night's job and Steelman, after he left you, called Guzik. Chapman had gone back and was manning the tap to see if anything would be said about our aborted raid and he heard Steelman tell Guzik what a time he had keeping you off the place as long as he did."

It came back to me then in little snatches. Steelman blaming the birds or the wind for dislodging the matches I had planted in the crack of the door. Steelman insisting that there was nothing there and that we were wasting our time. Steelman asking finally that we make sure before calling in the crew for a raid that might make "chumps" out of us. And all the time he was trying to collect for both of us.

"I'll be damned," I muttered.

Froelich sat back wearily.

"We picked up Steelman this morning and he confessed everything. He also cleared you completely of any knowledge or complicity. I'm damned glad it turned out this way for you, Paul."

"Me, too," I added thankfully. "But what's going to happen to Steelman?"

"He's resigning," Froelich said, wearing a worried look. "I half think that we should prosecute him. But our outfit is new here and we've got a big job to do. We'll need every ounce of public respect we can get if we are to expect any help from honest people. If this got out, that one of our crew had turned crooked already, it might ruin us for good. So, I figure that the best thing to do is kick him out and keep it off the record."

I was, in a way, glad for Steelman. You don't work with a man under such conditions without developing, if not a fondness, at least some sort of regard for him.

"So there it is," Froelich brought me out of my reverie. "And let me say again, Paul, that I'm damned glad you're out from under and, when I consider your record, I think we all owe you an apology."

I shrugged. "Forget it. Sometimes it's damned difficult

to nail the right man. I remember one time when I was on a spot separating the guilty from the innocent."

Froelich, obviously interested, asked me what had happened.

"Well, we made a raid in the mountains one night and picked up two guys running a big still," I told him. "It was dark as hell and the guy I collared asked me for a light for his cigaret. I had a good look at him but, just as I blew out the match, damned if he didn't bolt into the darkness and get away.

"We picked him up later," I recounted, "but when the case came to trial the defense had his three brothers on hand. They were alike as four peas in a pod and the defense attorney defied me to pick out the one I had collared on a night that was as dark as pitch. But I got a conviction."

Froelich leaned forward and asked, "How was it possible?"

"Easy," I grinned. "The guy whose cigaret I lit had blue eyes. All three of the other brothers had brown eyes."

His laugh followed me out of the office. And, after the way I had come out of this jam, I wore a big smile, too.

CHAPTER 4

That very night of the day on which I had been cleared, we all received an emergency summons for a raid on a brewery whose location Chapman had discovered through the phone tap on the Wabash Hotel.

One of the hoods had telephoned the need for a rush order of one hundred barrels of beer for "an outside source," the Capone operation being so large that it obviously was supplying adjacent areas when they ran short of liquid supplies.

"All right," said someone in authority at the Wabash, "send them down to Lumber Street."

"Where?"

"Lumber Street, you dope. 2271 Lumber Street."

The irony of it was that it was only five blocks from the dry hole we had hit when Steelman sold out Leeson's raid.

"Probably the same plant," Froelich commented. "So we get it now instead of a few weeks ago."

We hit it at about 10:30 that night and received quite a surprise. Leeson and I, leading the attack on the back entrance, had no trouble tearing down a flimsy wooden door.

But there, still confronting us, was another door and this one was made of steel. We hacked at it momentarily with an axe and a crowbar, causing a terrific din, and then Leeson panted impatiently: "Stand back."

The booming echo of Joe's .45 thundered through the alley as he shot through the lock and shouldered open the

50

door. There was the same clanging from the double doors in the front followed by the echo of gunfire and I knew as we pushed inside that there were steel doors there, too, and that the others were shooting their way in also.

Bursting in with drawn guns, not knowing what to expect, we saw a tremendously large, well-lighted room in which gigantic brewing vats lined one wall. The sour odor of mash permeated the air and two large trucks stood on the concrete floor, each partially loaded with barrels of beer.

But there wasn't a soul in sight.

Records of the Prohibition Bureau showed that not a single person ever had been arrested up to this time in a raid on a Capone brewery. Much of this was due to "protection" tipoffs which gave the hoodlums time to escape in the infrequent times they had been raided. There had been no tipoff this time, we were confident because of the evidences of sudden flight, including several cigaret butts still burning on the floor, but this was to be no exception as far as arrests were concerned.

The reason for their escape posed no problem.

A set of wooden stairs led to a trap door in the roof. The hatch still stood open. Lahart charged up the steps but came back shortly in disgust.

"They obviously escaped over the roofs of some other buildings," he grimaced. "They're long gone from here."

Still, we had accomplished something. For we had confiscated two almost new trucks, nineteen 1,500-gallon vats and 140 barrels of beer ready for distribution. Fourteen of the vats were filled with mash and the remaining five were cooling tanks filled with beer ready for barreling and distribution. We estimated the plant could produce one hundred barrels a day and set its value at $75,000.

The rugged and raging Leeson still wasn't satisfied. He took an axe and savagely whacked a hole in one of the huge vats, causing a stream of beer to cascade forth onto the floor.

"Dammit," he roared, "I wanted to grab these bastards and let 'em know that we really mean business."

We posted a guard while Chapman went to find a phone and call the contract crew to come and dismantle the plant. These contract men, as they were called, worked for a trucking and moving concern from whom we had obtained a bid on any dismantling work we might have. Low bidder had been a husky roughneck named Barney Doyle and it wasn't long before he showed up with his crew and began to take the plant apart.

"Not a bad start," Froelich enthused at a meeting the next morning. "True, we didn't make any arrests. But we did put an impressive dent in their operation and also let them know that we mean business. Still, we're going to have to figure out some way to counteract that steel door defense. They're certain to put them up at all their operations now."

The studious Chapman had the answer.

"I've been giving that a great deal of thought," he said in his scholarly manner. "I think if we took a ten-ton truck and mounted a large steel bumper on the front of it, something like a giant snow plow, we could crack right through any such doors and nail them in the act before they had a chance to escape."

Froelich's eyes lit up at the suggestion.

"Not only that," grunted big Joe Leeson, "we've got to stop up all the rat holes so they can't possibly get away."

"Well," Chapman continued, "we can carry our own scaling ladders on the truck. "Just before we hit a place, we can cover the roof as well as any ground floor exits."

"A fine idea," Froelich enthused and, turning to Chapman, added: "Lyle, you've got a free hand to come up with the kind of a truck you've suggested."

As the meeting broke up, Froelich asked me and Leeson to stay behind.

"Paul," he said, "I'd like to see you and Leeson team up now. Chapman, with whom he has been working, is getting snowed under with vitally necessary paper work. With Steelman gone, that leaves you both at loose ends. What do you think?"

Looking at the muscular, rock-hard Leeson, I nodded my satisfaction. It would be good to have a man with his strength handy in what undoubtedly was shaping up ahead of us now that the mob was fully warned that we were really out to get them.

"Suits me fine," Leeson approved.

"Fine," Froelich repeated. "And by the way, do either of you know any other agents whose absolute honesty you can guarantee? I think we're going to need a little more firepower."

Leeson, who had come out of touch-and-go Detroit, shook his head slowly from side to side.

My mind went over those I knew in the southern division. There were a number of them, including my South Carolina sidekick, Austin, who I knew to be completely honest and above suspicion. But I didn't think they'd appreciate duty in Chicago.

"There's one I can think of who would fill the bill and like the assignment," I proposed. "Mike King in Richmond."

King, I told him, was a handsome, drawling Virginian who was by way of being a legend among the prohibition men in the south. He was a dedicated and fearless agent with an impeccable reputation.

"Fine, I'll see about him," Froelich nodded.

Less than a week later King showed up as a replacement for Steelman. It was a trade, I knew, in which we had gotten much the best of the deal.

Leeson and I meanwhile had begun what was to be a longtime partnership and it almost opened with a bang—a fatal bang of gunfire.

I had picked him up the afternoon after Froelich assigned us to work together, as we did most of our work in the late afternoon and during the hours of darkness. Before going to his apartment I had traded in my old .45 on a snubnosed .38. The .45 was too heavy for constant wear and the .38 felt much more comfortable in my shoulder holster.

"Got a new gun," I told Leeson as we drove away from his place. "I've always used a .45 but it was too bulky. So I picked up a .38."

Leeson, as I have said, was an extremely powerful man and even the heavy .45 automatic he used looked like a toy in his massive hands.

"I'm a .45 man myself," he said. "Let me see your popgun."

At just about that time we pulled up to a traffic light. As the car stopped, I reached in and drew my .38 and swept my arm toward him.

"Drop it," Joe barked out of the side of his mouth. His face was impassive and he kept a steady stare straight ahead.

I didn't question him. I dropped it. The gun bounced off his knee and fell on the floorboards.

"What the hell. . . ." I started to say as the light changed.

"Look alongside us," Joe grunted, with an almost imperceptible jerk of his head out his side of the window.

I looked and must have turned white.

In stopping at the light, I had pulled up beside an armored money truck. The guard peering through the porthole had seen me draw my gun.

He had a tommygun sticking through the slot and aimed squarely at us!

"Whew!" I expelled my breath as the light turned and I gunned our car out ahead of the armored truck.

The imperturbable Leeson just grinned at me. To him it was a huge joke.

"Imagine if that guy had cut loose," he roared. "I can see the headlines now: 'Two Prohibition Agents Killed Trying To Rob Armored Car.' "

"Very, very funny," I said weakly over his booming laughter.

I had always wondered why Leeson was so fiercely relentless in his pursuit of hoodlums. As I said, with me it was an exciting, adventurous job and I didn't particularly hate those on the other side of the law, especially in view of the fact that I liked to take a drink or two myself. But with Leeson it was different. I found, the more time I spent with him, that with Joe it was a fixation which he carried on with all the fervor of a crusade.

He told me the reason one night as we sat in the car keeping watch on a garage loading platform which he had spotted earlier and thought looked suspicious because of the number of trucks which came and went each night. His voice was gruff and seething with hate as the words tumbled out of him.

"Those bastards," he grunted. "I'd like to nail every one of them to the mast."

"You sure take it hard, Joe," I remarked.

"Yeah," he said harshly, "I do. So would you if you were in my shoes."

"I couldn't fill 'em," I quipped.

"I'm not kidding," he said. "You know, Paul, I don't have a thing against booze and drinking. I can handle my share of it. After all, I spent a hitch in the navy and did my time in the hole stoking boilers. We had a real two-fisted bunch of guys. We helped keep a lot of joints in business and when we busted 'em up it was just for the hell of it."

I let him talk.

"We had just got back into Dago," he went on, using sailor parlance for San Diego, "when I got the word that my kid brother, Larry, had been found dead in a gutter in Detroit. My time was up so, instead of signing up for another hitch as I had expected to do, I hit out for home. Nobody could tell me what had happened. The cops had it marked as an unsolved case. No leads; no nothing."

Leeson's voice took on a cold, thin edge.

"The cops hadn't tried very hard. It was a cold trail by the time I got there yet, even at that late date, I was able to nose around and find out a few things."

Leeson was silent for a few moments. Then he went on.

"Larry was no angel. The kid had been mixed up in a couple of deals. But it wasn't anything real serious. Anyhow, I kept poking around and I found out he had been in a hassle with a bootlegger named Vito Bellardi over some girl.

"This punk thought he was a real big-timer," Joe almost whispered, lost in his thoughts. "I had to beat hell out of a couple of guys but I found out that Bellardi had knocked Larry off. Now, I asked myself, what's the best way to make this bum bleed? Put him out of business. So I joined the Prohibition Bureau and I made this bastard my number one target."

Joe paused and I asked, "What happened?"

"I spread the word around that I was the one who was after him," Joe said with obvious satisfaction. "He came looking for me."

"Then?" I queried softly.

"I killed him!"

There was a long silence. At last Joe spoke again, his voice low and intense.

"That's why I hate hoods, Paul. I'm sorry but it's the way it has to be. Every time I get a crack at them I'm gonna go all out. Maybe, that way, I can save somebody else's kid brother."

I reached over and shook him by the shoulder.

"Joe," I said softly, "I'm with you."

So did we come together and from that night forward Joe Leeson and I were a team that hell, high water or Herbert Hoover couldn't have broken up.

Yet there was a kind of a humorous outcome to that evening which welded us together. We had been sitting there almost an hour in utter silence, watching that truck loading platform when a van rumbled up and started backing in.

"Let's give it a rumble," Joe said suddenly.

Simultaneously we leaped from the car, raced along the sidewalk and across the street to the loading platform. One guy in coveralls was just letting down the overhead door but we ducked under it and Leeson crashed against him and knocked him down.

"Sorry, buddy," he said solicitously, yanking the amazed character to his feet and hustling him along in front of us. "We just want to take a quick look."

One look was enough. The entire garage was stacked high with cases of imported Canadian beer.

Leeson was jubilant as we lined up the attendant, the driver and two loaders against the wall.

"High-class stuff. Imported. Boy, they must get a pretty penny for this."

It was good stuff. I know because, there being so much evidence, Joe and I put a couple of cases in the back of our car and subsequently took it home.

"Let's just sit around here a while," Joe said. "I've got a feeling that with all this grade-A beer on hand we may have a few more customers."

We herded the four prisoners into a tiny, glass-windowed office in a rear corner of the garage and I stood watch over them.

"Give me your coveralls," Joe directed the man he had flattened.

"Hell," the guy yelped, "I ain't got nothin' on underneath."

"Good, we'll see what kind of a man you are," Joe grinned wickedly.

"Get 'em off or I'll really give you some lumps."

Hastily if reluctantly the man shed his coveralls. He was right. He didn't have anything on underneath.

"No wonder he's embarrassed," Joe said scathingly as the man huddled in a corner of the little room.

In the course of the next couple of hours, two more huge vans appeared. They were ceremoniously guided in their backing-in parking operations by the coverall-garbed Leeson, and the drivers then were ushered unceremoniously into the back to join the other prisoners.

"Well, I guess that's about it for the night," Joe said finally. "Call the paddy wagon from the local precinct to pick up these jerks and I'll wait here until I can get the contract men to pick up the trucks."

When the patrol wagon arrived and the prisoners were locked safely inside I jumped into our car and followed the police van to the local precinct station.

"Robsky, Prohibition Bureau," I told the sergeant on duty at the desk. "I need a receipt for these prisoners."

While we were talking I glanced at the ledger in which the prisoners had been booked. It handed me a real laugh.

"This one guy is a real joker," I told the sergeant. "Look here."

The sergeant read it and started swearing.

One prisoner had given, as his own, the name of the Chicago Police Commissioner.

"Get another name from that guy," the sergeant told the patrolman who had put them in the tank. "You know better than that, you dope."

Shortly thereafter the patrolman returned and handed the sergeant a slip. Once more the sergeant cut loose with a string of oaths.

"Now he gave you the name of the former commissioner of police," he roared. "Shake that son of a bitch up and get his real handle."

The patrolman slammed angrily into the cell block and came back a few minutes later with another slip of paper. The sergeant gave it a quick look, entered the name in the book, and handed me a receipt. He was telling me a story and, absent-mindedly, I stuffed the receipt into my pocket without looking at the name the impudent prisoner had given. Then, it being quite late and being bushed from all the waiting and resultant action, I headed home and went to bed.

The shrill of the telephone brought me wide awake with the sun streaming in the windows. I groped for the phone.

"Robsky," I said sleepily.

Froelich's voice came over the wire.

"Hello, Paul. I'm glad to see you out on bail."

"What in hell are you talking about?"

Froelich laughed heartily. "Get a morning paper and read about the raid pulled off by, and I quote, Prohibition Agent Leeson." With that he hung up.

My curiosity aroused, I dressed and went down to the corner and bought the morning paper. It was right there on page one, about how Leeson had apprehended six men engaged in the movement of illicit alcohol and confiscated three trucks and ten thousand dollars worth of imported beer. I didn't see anything humorous in that. But then my eyes took in the list of the defendants and there, in bold-face type which listed those who had been apprehended, it read:

"Paul Robsky, 4052 Sheridan Road."

The wise-guy prisoner of the night before, who first had given the names of the former and present commissioners of police, in a third try had given my name. I had been too preoccupied to read it when the patrolman handed it to the desk sergeant and my name had been entered as one of those booked. What puzzled me, and what I never have been able to find out, was how the guy had my name let alone my correct address.

Leeson ribbed me unmercifully when I picked him up that evening.

"I don't know whether I should be seen riding around with a liquor-law violator," he chuckled.

"Well, things aren't always what they seem," I retorted with a grin.

"How's that?"

"One time down in the mountains," I told him, "we raided a spot and as we swarmed down on the place with our guns ready a Negro saw us and started to run for all he was worth. I ran him down but he protested his innocence and we were finally satisfied that he was telling the truth.

"I asked him why he had started to run and he said 'To tell you the truth, boss, when I sees all those guns—I just hadda run.'"

Leeson chortled and said mockingly:

"Well, from now on watch the company you keep."

I meant it when I said I sure would. For it wouldn't be very funny if my folks or their friends saw that in the paper back in Galesburg.

CHAPTER 5

Given a free hand by Froelich, the erudite Chapman had turned all his efforts toward producing the kind of a truck we knew we would need to crack open the heavily reinforced doors of the alerted Capone breweries.

The work had been done secretly at the garage of one of Chapman's closest friends, a man whose integrity was above question. And now Lyle spread the word among us that we all were invited to the very private "by invitation only" unveiling. When the time came, we were amazed at what we saw.

"Holy Moses," Leeson exclaimed as we inspected Chapman's creation. "It looks like a cross between an army tank and a freight car."

Chapman had, without question, done an excellent job. Ironically, he had taken one of the finest of the trucks we had confiscated from the mob and turned it into a juggernaut which would be used against the underworld.

As far as I could see, nothing had been left undone. The back had been stripped down and there was a rack equipped with scaling ladders, the ends of them padded so that they wouldn't make the slightest sound when run up against the side of a building. And wrapped around the front, with a pointed prow like a battleship, was a massive steel bumper which promised to shatter anything which stood in its way. There even were handles welded at strategic spots on the inside of the cab so that those riding in it would have protective handholds during the moment of impact.

"It looks all right but we'll have to see how it works

out," Chapman cautioned, although he was obviously pleased.

We weren't long in putting it to the test.

It was only a day or two later that Lahart and Seager came up with what was undoubtedly a large brewery on Cicero Avenue. They had kept it under surveillance long enough to know that it was a swinging operation and, such was the vigilant prudence which the mob was beginning to practice, the brewery apparently operated only from four to six o'clock in the morning.

"I guess," said Lahart when Froelich called us in for a briefing, "that they don't think any prohibition agent alive would work at such an ungodly hour."

We planned the raid with extreme care, profiting from our past mistakes. This one we meant to hit from front, rear—and top—all at the same instant.

Chapman, as its creator, was given what I privately considered the rather dubious honor of driving the truck through the front doors. It could, I conjectured, become a test case between the irresistible force and the immovable object. I found myself rather amazed that the quiet, scholarly looking Chapman seemed to be enjoying the prospect of what might possibly develop into an oversized automobile accident.

Leeson and I were assigned to the role of scaling the building and closing off that favored avenue of escape while the rest of the squad was split up, some to crash in from the rear and others to flank the truck and follow it in on foot.

We all were in hidden positions by four o'clock in the morning and remained concealed as several trucks drove up to the sprawling building, flicked their lights and drove in through the quickly opened and hastily closed doors.

Chapman had his truck concealed in a bisecting alley a half a block away and, with the raid set for five a.m., Leeson and I waited in tense silence with Chapman and Ness, who was riding with him.

At times like this I could feel my pulse pounding and

we checked our watches constantly, anxious for the action to begin.

After what seemed like hours of waiting, it was 4:55 and Leeson whispered hoarsely: "Let's get our ladder and get going."

Noiselessly we lifted it down from the back of the truck and, with one of us at each end, darted up a back alley and approached the brewery from the rear. I stiffened as I spotted two shadowy shapes in an opaque opening between two buildings, but sighed with relief as I perceived that is was Lahart and Seager, who were to lead the attack on the rear. Lahart raised one arm in silent salutation but Seager remained motionless.

"Up with it," Leeson breathed softly as we reached the side of the building.

We hoisted the ladder, wordlessly thanking Chapman's insight in padding it so ingeniously as it rested soundlessly against the building. Then we were scrambling up the rungs to the flat, tar-papered roof.

"Careful," Leeson whispered, "so we don't make any noise and tip them off."

Looking about, I saw a skylight. It gave off only a faint glow and I knew that the glass had been covered with black paint. Just beyond it loomed a rooftop doorway, standing at attention like a misplaced subway kiosk.

"You take one side and I'll take the other," I told Joe.

We didn't have long to wait. There was the roaring rumble of our experimental truck as Chapman gunned it down the street. The tires screamed as it swung in toward the double doors and Chapman really gunned the motor. Then came a ripping, rending crash and the shrill scream of tortured metal. We had guessed right. There was another steel door inside the wooden one. As the echo died away, I could hear a pounding below us and at the rear of the building as Lahart and Seager went into action breaking in from that direction. Muffled yells echoed up through the skylight and the pounding of footsteps sounded inside the doorway we guarded.

"Here we go," Joe said in a stage whisper.

The door was flung open and a hatless figure was outlined in the light from below. Leeson stepped out swiftly,
stuck out his leg and tripped the fleeing man as he
plunged through the doorway. The hoodlum was as quick
as a panther, and just as deadly, for he rolled and came
up with a knife in his hand. Leeson lunged at him, caught
the wrist of his knife hand and they went down in a struggling heap.

Before I could spring to Joe's aid, however, another
figure pounded through the doorway.

"Hold it," I shouted. "This is a federal raid."

Instead of stopping, the man whipped out a pistol, fired
a shot which I heard whine past my head, and began to
sprint toward an adjoining rooftop. Meanwhile he loosed
another shot back over his shoulder. Instinctively I
snapped a shot at him with my .38. His figure jerked convulsively, took a few tottering steps and plunged through
the skylight. A scream slashed through the sound of shattered glass.

Whirling to go to Leeson's aid, I saw Joe rising with
the hoodlum in his grasp. He had disarmed the mobster
and as I started toward them, Joe drove a big, boney fist
to the man's jaw and the gangster wilted to the rooftop.
Stooping easily, Leeson picked up the hood with as much
effort as if he had been a rag doll, threw him over his
shoulder and motioned me ahead of him down the stairs.

This time I saw, as we descended the stairs, we had hit
the jackpot.

Our truck had done the job for which it had been
designed with a magnificent efficiency. The front doors
looked as if they had been blown open with a charge of
dynamite. A quick look showed me that the truck had
come through with no damage except a gleaming gash in
the steel bumper which glittered like a badge of honor.

And, for the first time in prohibition history, we had
captured prisoners in a raid on a Capone brewery.

Three of them stood lined up under Chapman's gun,
their hands in the air and sullen, defiant sneers on their

faces. Leeson strode over and dumped his still unconscious prisoner on the concrete floor at their feet.

"Here's another rat," he said. Then, turning to me, he
grinned and asked: "Where's the guy who took the
tumble through the skylight?"

I had been inspecting our haul, and it was a good one.
Seven huge 3,500-gallon vats stood in a row along one
side of the brewery and the three new trucks all had been
in the process of being loaded. Savoring our success, I
had forgotten all about the man I had winged.

"Cripes," I told Joe, "I don't know where the hell he
is."

My eyes darted up to the shattered skylight and Leeson
and I moved over to where the hoodlum would have had
to fall.

The hole was directly over one of those huge brewing
vats!

We walked around it but the gangster was nowhere in
sight. Joe looked at me and I looked at him. Then he
pointed an extended forefinger in jerky little motions
toward the vat.

"You mean . . . ?" I asked.

Joe nodded and smiled crookedly.

"Yeah, that's what I mean. The guy you winged has
got to be in there taking a bath."

"Hey, somebody bring a ladder off the truck," I yelled.

Lahart and Seager, who had entered through the rear,
brought one to us and Leeson and I ran it up against the
side of the vat.

I scrambled up and looked down into the foaming brew
inside the vat. Leeson had been right. The hood's body
was there, floating face down in the beer.

Leaning over the edge, I reached in and got a grip on
his collar and dragged the motionless form over to the
edge. It took all my strength, perched on the ladder as I
was, to hoist him gradually until his body was draped
over the edge.

"Okay," Leeson called up to me from below, where he

was standing with head thrown back watching. "Come on down, Paul, and I'll get that monkey."

Quickly I slid down the ladder and Leeson climbed up. It was no task for him, with his enormous strength, to lift the hoodlum under one arm and carry him back down. Then he laid the mobster on the floor.

"He's dead as a mackerel," Joe grunted.

He was, too. But, a subsequent autopsy showed, he hadn't died from my bullet. My shot had caught him in his shoulder.

The fall in some way, possibly in striking his head a glancing blow on the side of the vat, had knocked him unconscious.

He had drowned in the huge vat of beer.

The story of our successful raid, as well as the rather unusual manner in which the mobster had died, made headlines in all the newspapers. For this had been a real body blow to Capone. Not only had we knocked out a hundred-barrel-a-day brewery but we had captured his chief brewmaster, a surly arrogant man named Steve Svoboda.

"I'll be out before the ink is dry on the police blotter," he had bragged to us.

"Maybe so," retorted Leeson, "but we'll have you back in again and you're going to find out it's a costly proposition, both from the standpoint of money as well as time in the clink, to thumb your nose at Uncle Sam."

The publicity given our raid served as more than ample warning to the mob that we really meant business. Froelich was deeply concerned that there might well be violent reprisals.

His worry showed in his voice. "I want all of you men to be particularly careful from now on. Watch yourselves crossing the street." He laughed weakly at his ineffectual attempt to make a joke of his warning.

We weren't destined to face tommygun or "pineapple" yet. The mob resorted first to the method which never before had failed—the payoff.

Two days after the first successful use of our battering-ram truck, Leeson and I were stopped at a traffic light when a black sedan drew up beside us.

"You, Robsky," a swarthy man in the mob's traditional pearl-gray hat called. It was proof, I realized when I considered it later, that they had each one of us pegged by sight and name.

I looked over at him and tensed, Froelich's warning leaping into my mind. My hand darted inside my coat to my pistol and the mobster, catching the motion, held up a restraining hand.

"Wait a second," he said hurriedly. "I just want to give you something. And if you guys play your cards right, there'll be more every week."

With that, he reached into his lap and tossed something in through my window.

"Watch it," I snapped at Leeson, not having any idea what it was he had flung at us. Then my eyes popped as I shot a quick look at what Joe was holding.

It was a roll of bills big enough to choke a horse.

Anger showed in the set of Leeson's jaw, the knuckles of one big hand turning white as he clutched the roll of bills. His voice rasped with ill-controlled fury.

"Catch those bastards," he said as the car beside us pulled ahead, "and I'll make 'em eat this wad, bill by bill."

There was a car ahead of me and, as I tried to pull into the left lane to follow the mobsters who had thrown us the money, another machine drew up alongside us and kept me pinned in my lane. While we were held there, the other car sped away and, turning a corner, was lost to view. Two men in the car next to us grinned wickedly. They, too, wore pearl-gray hats and we knew that they were running interference so that the other car could get away without any possible pursuit from us.

"We oughta pull those guys over and beat hell out of 'em," Leeson growled.

I shook my head.

"You can't smack these guys around just because they're driving an automobile and got in our way."

Reluctantly, Joe agreed.

"No, I guess not. But I feel like doing it on general principles." Then he brightened and suggested slyly, "I bet we'd get away with it, too. They're sure fire to have records as long as your arm."

"Nothing doing," I restrained him. "Let's just take those good old American dollars and turn 'em over to Froelich. And, by the way, how much is in that wad?"

Joe unsnapped a large rubber band which held the roll together and let out a long, soft whistle as he thumbed through the bills.

"Junior," he said to me with wide eyes, "there is exactly two thousand clams here. Looks like we have attained quite a nuisance value in this fair city."

"Two thousand bucks," I repeated. "Wow!"

In a later day and age this would not seem like much money. But at that point our nation was writhing in the throes of the worst depression it ever had known. To each of us that roll clamped in Leeson's fist represented almost a year's salary. A man would be less than human if he didn't sit there looking at it and figuring all the things it could buy.

Yet I can honestly say that it never entered my mind, or Leeson's, that we should keep this blood money.

Driving to the federal building, we parked and went on up to Froelich's office.

"Here's a little donation for Uncle Sam," Joe said as he strode to Froelich's desk and tossed the roll of money down in front of the Assistant United States Attorney General. Froelich's eyes became round with surprise and his surprise showed in his tone.

"Where did this come from?"

"A little protection payoff from the mob for me and Joe," I grinned. "But we don't have enough spare time to spend it, so we thought maybe you'd know what to do with it."

"How much is in it?" Froelich asked.

"Two G's," Joe told him.

"I beg your pardon?"

Leeson chuckled.

"Sorry. Two thousand bucks."

"Oh," Froelich said. "Quite a sizable sum."

"You can say that again," Joe retorted.

"How did you get it?"

Tersely, Joe told him about the incident and how those who offered us the bribe had gotten away from us.

Froelich stared at the roll as if it had him hypnotized. From the way his eyes narrowed and he pursed his lips I knew that inside that shrewd head the wheels were spinning furiously.

"I've got it," he said suddenly.

"Got what?" I asked.

"How we can turn this to our advantage and let these people know that this is a war to the finish. Give me about an hour and then come back here to my office."

We left, both of us mystified as to what Froelich had up his well-tailored sleeve.

"Now what do you suppose that legal eagle has cooking in his mind?" Joe mused as we sat over a cup of coffee. I was puzzled, too. The best I could offer was a mystified "Search me."

When we returned to Froelich's office at the appointed time, the reception room was crowded. There were a number of cameras in evidence.

"What's this?" Joe quietly asked the girl behind the reception desk.

"Go right on in," she told us. "Mister Froelich well tell you."

We went inside and Froelich smiled at us with one of those cat-swallowed-the-canary looks.

"We're going to give the Prohibition Bureau, and the honest people in this town, the biggest shot in the arm they've had in years," he beamed. "You men are going to tell the newspapers just what happened. Believe me, it's big news when a law officer in this city turns in a mob payoff which is almost as much as he earns in an entire year."

Reporters listened to our story and asked numerous

questions. Cameras flashed and Joe, uncomfortable in the limelight, whispered to me, "Maybe we should have kept the damned money if it's gonna create all this excitement."

"Maybe so," I muttered, for, as the reporters left, I heard one of them say to another: "I'd hate to be in those guys' shoes when the syndicate reads about this."

They had, I knew, a deadly point. Such defiance of the syndicate was unheard of in this racket-ridden city where those who dared stand in the way of the mob were either paid off or knocked off. Our disclosure of the payoff attempt had to be quite a sensation.

It was, indeed. Front page stories across the nation headlined our contempt of the Capone mob.

One Chicago newspaper began its story:

"A special band of Prohibition agents have proved to Al Capone that its members are untouchable."

Emblazoned across the top of the story was the headline:

THE UNTOUCHABLES

Wire services snatched at the phrase and spread it to every corner of the country. Thus came into being the name by which we were to be known and one in which we took a tremendous personal pride.

Still, as we were to learn shortly, we didn't quite deserve this tribute—yet.

Because, in the next few weeks, we began once again to hit dry holes as we battered our way into breweries or drops which undoubtedly had been in operation. Yet, when we raided them, in most cases we found them to be empty or else disappointingly small.

Finally, after the third dry hole in a row, Froelich called the entire squad into his office to discuss the situation.

"Something is definitely wrong," he frowned, tugging furiously at his ear lobe.

The irrepressible Lahart, who was watching Froelich closely, pointed at the Assistant United States Attorney General and said "Maybe that's it."

"What?"

"The ear," Lahart replied. "We've got wire taps on them. Maybe they've got one on us in our office at the Transportation Building—and maybe even on your phone here."

Froelich snapped his fingers impatiently, sitting back and staring hard at the phone sitting silently erect on his desk.

"Why didn't I think of that sooner? Well, if that is the trouble, we'll soon check that out."

He picked up a pad from his desk and waved it at us.

"Maybe the answer, or part of it, is in here, too. These," he explained, "are Chapman's notes on the wire tap at the Wabash Hotel. Now, listen to this."

Froelich leafed through several pages and then, clearing his throat, began to read from the wire tap notes:

"Hello, Jake?"

"This is Fusco."

"Yes, Joe."

Fusco, I knew, was one of the top echelon members of the mob. I listened intently as Froelich continued reading from the pad.

"Jake, I've got something real hot."

"What about?"

"A little sugar investment that might save us a lot of trouble and headaches, as well as money in the long run."

All of us became even more quietly attentive. There was only one interpretation of "sugar." That meant the payoff. But we were to be disappointed. It showed in Froelich's voice, too, as he read on.

"Wait a minute, Joe. That's entirely in Ralph's hands at the moment. You'd better call him at the Montmartre."

"Well . . . okay. I'll talk to you later."

Froelich threw the pad onto the top of his desk with an irritated gesture.

"We might have learned something there but, unfortunately we didn't. With Al Capone still out of town, his brother Ralph seems to be pulling the big strings right now, if we take Guzik's own word for it. But it appears to me as if they have a new source of information."

I looked quickly around at the others, for a tense atmosphere had developed in the room as we all digested this information. Leeson, I saw, was running his eyes over them, too. The usually gay Lahart was tight-lipped and silent. Ness was staring at Froelich, looking less the boyish collegian than ever. Seager was as stonily impassive as ever.

Chapman, frowning, stared at the carpet. Mike King, ever at ease, was the only one who seemed relaxed. Arnold Grant, eyes narrowed, was stroking that pencil-line Hollywood moustache with restless fingers and slender Jim Taylor gazed stonily out of the window.

I couldn't bring myself to believe that any one of these men could sell us out. It had to be a tap on our own lines, I reasoned.

Froelich's voice interrupted my inspection of the other members of our group.

"Now, let's not jump to conclusions. We don't know who this might be that they're talking about. But it's obvious that they have found an important source of information."

Froelich wasn't tipping his hand to anyone. The meeting broke up without any concrete action but, as we all prepared to leave, he asked Leeson, Lahart, Ness and me to stay "for a few minutes on another matter."

When the rest had gone he broke the silence, a grim edge in his voice.

"Gentlemen, I hate to say this, but I think that there's a distinct possibility the mob may have gotten to one of our squad. Now, considering the fine progress we have made and the growing reputation of 'The Untouchables,' I don't want all this ruined. One misstep and we could destroy everything we have accomplished. Which is why, number one, I don't want to bring in a 'torpedo' from outside as we did before."

We waited and, after a few seconds, Froelich continued.

"What I think we're going to have to do is get a tap on Ralph Capone at the Montmartre. You four all have proved yourselves beyond any thought of defection and please don't jump to the conclusion that I have anything but the highest regard for the others. It's simply that somewhere there has to be a leak and I think we should play this as close to the vest as possible until we find out where it might be. But understand, I'm not saying that it has to be one of us."

Leeson broke into the conversation, his voice tight.

"What do you suggest?"

Froelich nodded toward Ness.

"Eliot and I have discussed this at some length. It's going to be a man-sized job to get that tap on the Montmartre. We've already staked out the place and I can tell you that it's as heavily guarded as the United States mint, maybe more so.

"Our observations have shown," he continued, "that both the front and rear always have a certain quota of the mob in attendance. We also have checked with private sources in the telephone company on which we can depend with extreme confidence. That's where the difficulty lies. The terminal box on which we must make the tap is located on a pole in the alley right behind the back door of the Montmartre and there are always a couple of the mob on guard there."

Froelich tented his fingers, a favorite gesture, and, as he paused for breath, Leeson grunted, "So what do we do?" Froelich smiled thinly at his impatience.

"First of all, for obvious reasons, I'd like to keep what we are going to do confidential among those of us who are here right now. I don't think I have to tell you why."

He didn't. We were out to trap the informer among us, if there was one.

"Secondly," Froelich continued, swinging around and bobbing his head in my direction, "Paul is going back to school briefly and then he'll make the tap while the rest of the squad draws off the mob's watchdogs on a wild goose chase."

Leeson interrupted again.

"Why Paul?"

It gave me a warm feeling which offset the cold chill I felt at the prospect of playing clay pigeon at the top of a telephone pole. For I knew that Joe was considering me in the same light.

"Paul served in the signal corps in the army," Froelich said, asking me in an aside "That right?"

I nodded.

"Well," he went on, "this is a ticklish job because this is a new type of terminal box, having some 150 terminals to be bridged before we can make the right connection. Paul, having some familiarity with this type of thing, is going to spend a few days with a telephone company expert to get the hang of things. Then he'll know what to do."

There was only one drawback, as Froelich outlined the plan. We would have to have someone on the inside whose voice was familiar to me so that I would recognize it while racking the board. This was where Lahart came in. Froelich explained that Marty, in disguise, was going undercover as an out-of-town hoodlum visiting Chicago because he was "hot" somewhere else.

Froelich, with his painstaking attention to detail, already had planned Marty's disguise as a flashily dressed mobster from the west coast. It would be seen to by the Justice Department that phony wanted broadsides of him would get into the right—or wrong—hands in Chicago.

"I've even obtained a membership card for him to get him inside the Montmartre," Froelich explained. "He shouldn't have any trouble getting to use the telephone there at the time we set for the raid. And, in case there are any suspicions of him and anybody listens in, he'll be talking to a lady—I believe the mobsters refer to them as 'broads'—who is the widow of a Justice Department agent and has just moved back to Chicago.

"When Marty is ready," Froelich summed up, "he'll call the lady, whom we'll refer to as 'Edna,' as if for a date the next night at eight o'clock. We'll move in whatever day the date happens to be for—but four hours earlier—at which time he'll be calling her to remind her to be on time. That way Paul can recognize his voice."

Thus the trap was laid, with Marty and me as bait. Personally, I felt like a tasty piece of cheese about to be devoured by a horde of rats.

The next few days I spent with a chief telephone company technician named Alan Sargent. Under his tutelage I learned the intricacies of the complicated terminal boxes such as the one behind the Montmartre. And I filled my hands with splinters clambering up and down telephone poles until I was sufficiently accomplished with the lineman's spikes which would be necessary on the job facing me.

We did another thing.

Sargent and I ran a check on Froelich's telephone line at the federal building and also on our squad lines into the Transportation Building.

Every one of them was tapped.

"It doesn't surprise me," Sargent shrugged. "We've had a number of able men who have quit and gone to work for the mob."

We cleared our own lines and Sargent promised to keep them that way in the future even if it required a daily check.

"Which I'm quite certain it will," he grinned. "They won't quit easy."

Finally the day came when he told me that I knew all he could teach me for the job I had ahead of me. I felt like I was walking the last mile as I trudged into Froelich's office and told him "I'm ready whenever you are."

I had to sweat it out several more days, however. Lahart was working his way cautiously into the confidence of those in the Montmartre and, while all was going well, he hadn't yet given his "broad" the pre-planned code message.

But at last those of us on the inside, Leeson, Chapman, Ness and I, were summoned hastily to Froelich's office.

"It's on," the energetic Froelich said with a slight trace of nervousness. "Lahart called 'Edna' today—from the

Montmartre—and made a date with her for eight o'clock tomorrow night. He even had some hoodlum 'pal' of his talk to her and help him with his sales pitch.

"So," he made that perpetual steeple with his fingertips, "we hit it at four o'clock tomorrow afternoon."

"Great," I said, "but what happens to those two hoods guarding the back door? I'm not exactly unknown to those monkeys."

Froelich held up a restraining hand.

"That's where the rest of the squad comes in, even though they don't have any inkling of what's taking place. I'll call you all in here tomorrow morning and you men show up with the rest as if you don't know anything, either. Then I'll say I've decided on a show of strength to throw a little scare into the mob. Just go along with me when the time comes."

I had a little trouble sleeping that night. Leeson sat up with me quite late while we killed off the remainder of a very fine quart of imported whiskey, a bit of evidence from a raided "drop" which in some strange manner hadn't been destroyed until we personally got around to it. We finally accomplished the job, with water chasers.

CHAPTER 6

Looking back on the violent events which happened during those days in Chicago, I was to marvel often at the fact that any of us survived our deadly, running battle with the mob. And yet nothing surpasses, in retrospective chills, the thought of making that wire tap at the Montmartre and sitting at the top of that pole like a clay pigeon in a shooting gallery.

Just thinking about it gave me the creeps as I dressed the morning after Froelich had advised us that we would move in this very day. We had been ordered to report to his office at two o'clock in the afternoon and it seemed as if the hours never would pass.

"That way," Froelich had explained, "we'll all be together until the plan is put into operation and, if there is a defector among us, he'll not be able to tip off the mob as to what's going on in any manner whatsoever."

The time finally came and we were all gathered once again in the Assistant United States Attorney General's office. He appeared as urbane and poised as ever and, I conjectured somewhat ruefully, why shouldn't he be calm. After all, I was first prize in this turkey shoot if anything went wrong.

Froelich carried off his part with extreme finesse.

"Men, I understand from a private source that certain top men in the mob have been sounding off about how they're going to run us right off the streets. I don't have to tell you that we are getting quite a vaunted reputation as fearless gangbusters. It occurred to me that it might be a good idea to put on a sort of parade in the vicinity of the

Montmartre, Ralph Capone's headquarters, just to let
them and anybody else who might be interested know
how easy we are to find if anybody really wants us."

Chapman chimed in quickly.

"It sounds like a good idea to me."

"Me, too," Leeson threw his support to the plan, giving
those who weren't in on the scheme the idea that it was a
sudden suggestion which pleased him.

"Fine," Froelich said. "After all, you are the ones taking the risks and I wondered whether I might be pre-
suming too much from the safety of my office."

"That's our job," I told him. "Personally, I'll be glad to
go along."

Froelich waved a casual hand.

"I've got something else I want you and Ness to do for
me today," he said, clearing us from being sent out with
the others. "Just routine, and I hate to see you miss the
fun. But there is a certain amount of paper work that has
to be accomplished.

"And," he added, jolting me a bit, "Leeson asked
several days ago for the rest of the day off. Therefore he
won't be with us, either."

I shot a look at Joe, but he ignored my glance and, sitting relaxed in his chair, kept his eyes pinned on Froelich.

"So," Froelich continued, "I want King, Grant and
Taylor to take the open touring car and circle the block in
front of the Montmartre starting at about 3:30 p.m. Then
I'd like Chapman and Seager to drive up in front of the
Montmartre at 3:45 and sit there openly watching it for
about five minutes. At 3:50 precisely, they'll start touring
the adjacent blocks slowly as if looking for something.

"Now," he said, "the mob should spot you without any
difficulty and I'm certain they'll start tailing you wherever
you go. Ignore them—but keep a couple of tommyguns
and sawed-off shotguns in plain sight so they'll know
you're ready for business."

"You mean that's all we're supposed to do?" asked
Grant, fingering that pencil-line moustache as usual.

"That's all," Froelich answered quietly. "All I want is

for them to get the idea that we're around, watchful, waiting and available any time they feel like they want trouble."

The slender Taylor seemed mystified.

"It all doesn't make much sense to me," he said.

Froelich smiled.

"Just chalk it up as being one of my peculiarities," he replied. "I'm damned proud of you men and while this may be just a sop to my vanity, this is the way I'd like it to be. As a matter of fact, I'd like to ride along."

"It's okay by me," Taylor shrugged.

"Now, on this matter I have for Robsky and Ness . . ." Froelich began, checking himself and telling Chapman, "why don't the rest of you go down for a cup of coffee?"

Cognizant of the setup, Chapman rose with alacrity and led the others out. Nobody would get to a phone with him along, I knew, and, even if they did, there wasn't much they could reveal. Leeson went along with them, waving me a quick "So long. See you tomorrow."

If it had been almost anyone else, I'd have suspected him being "off" on this day. But not Joe.

When they had gone, leaving Ness and me with Froelich, the counselor turned to me and asked:

"Are you all set?"

I nodded.

"I'm as ready as I'll ever be."

"Are you sure you can make the tap?"

"If Lahart is on that phone inside the Montmartre, I'll make it—barring interference from below."

"Fine," Froelich said with a tone of relief in his voice. "All right, why don't you two take off and get yourselves in position. I'm quite certain that our caravan in front will draw the guards away from the back."

I grinned wryly.

"I sure hope you're right. And I also hope you keep them away until I at least get down off that pole."

We left, Ness and I, and as the time neared for us to be in position, we parked in the block behind the Montmartre and ducked into an alleyway which bisected the cobbled alley in the rear of the club. Under my arm I carried the tools of my new trade: coveralls and the broad leather belt and spikes of a telephone company lineman.

Acting as casually as possible we walked through the alleyway and, coming to the alley behind the Montmartre, peered cautiously around the corner of a high broad fence. It was as we knew it would be. Two of the pearl-gray hats, as we always referred to the Capone mobsters, lounged at the back entrance to the mob's command post smoking cigarets. A new sedan stood nearby. We ducked back into the protective shadows of the narrow alleyway and, being careful not to make the slightest sound, I unrolled my gear, climbed into the coveralls and strapped on the belt and the needlepointed climbing spikes. Then we huddled against the wall, with less than five minutes to wait before the four o'clock "parade" in front of the Montmartre which, we desperately hoped, would draw off these rear-entrance guards.

The minutes ticked past with measured cadence and, when my watch showed it to be five minutes past four o'clock, in a low voice I asked Ness:

"Any action out there yet?"

Cautiously he peered around the corner.

"Nothing," he said bitterly. "Not a damned thing."

We hunkered on our heels in the shadows and another five minutes crawled past.

"Wait a minute," he cautioned suddenly. "I hear something."

I heard it, too, the slam of a door, the pounding of feet and the start of a car motor. There was the staccato slamming of car doors and we pressed back against the wall of the trash-littered alleyway as the sedan roared past us with a whine of tortured rubber from the tires.

"All clear," Ness said shortly. "Let's go."

He moved noiselessly ahead of me and I flinched involuntarily as the spikes I was wearing clanked with the loud voice of doom on the alley cobblestones. No one was in sight but I was panting, and dashed a film of sweat off my forehead with the back of one hand despite the coolness of the late afternoon, as I halted at the base of the pole and looked up at the large black terminal box outlined against the sky. It seemed to be miles away but, clamping my lips together and throwing one quick look at the unguarded back door of the Montmartre, I jammed my spikes into the pole and started my ascent.

The higher I reached the more naked I felt, even though the figure of Ness standing tensely below me with drawn gun offered a certain amount of solace. Then I became absorbed in the task at hand.

Whipping my belt around the pole and securing it, I stamped my spikes in securely and leaned back against the webbing around my waist. The door to the terminal box jammed momentarily but I pried it open and went to work racking the board.

Nothing.

There were a few voices here and there but nowhere could I pick up Lahart's voice. Fighting back a rising panic, I started over all the terminals once again, steeling myself against looking down to see if anyone was approaching. Then, suddenly, there was Lahart's familiar voice.

". . . and don't forget, baby, when I say eight o'clock, I mean eight o'clock right on the button."

Quickly I made the bridge, fingers flying. Then, carefully, I closed the terminal box and slid rapidly down the pole, cursing as I picked up another handful of splinters.

"Okay," I snapped, "let's get the hell out of here while we're all in one piece."

We sprinted for the alleyway and I waited until we were almost to the car before I stopped to shed my gear.

"Phew," I breathed. "I still can't get over thinking what would have happened if those monkeys had come back while I still was up there at the top of the pole."

Ness grinned and his voice was calm. "Why Paul, I had this little old .38 all ready."

"Big deal," I laughed. "So there'd have been two dead men, instead of one."

We drove back to report the success of our mission to Froelich and had to wait for him to return.

"It really was quite a lot of fun," he said as he breezed in much like a schoolboy who had been making dynamite in a chemistry lab. "You should have seen them. They were all around us."

"Dandy," I told him with a wry smile. "Better you than me."

We were talking of how it had gone when the door opened and Leeson walked in. He slumped into a chair, big shoulders thrown back, and looked at me with a whitetoothed grin. "Hey," I said, "I thought you were off somewhere."

"You sure looked like a monkey on a stick," he said.

"What do you mean . . . ?"

Froelich laughed.

"Joe didn't want me to tell you about it," he smiled, "but he was kind of worried about you. So this week he rented a room looking out over the back alley right behind the Montmartre."

"Yeah," Joe grunted in obvious embarrassment. "I was sitting up there with a chopper. And God help the guy who had come along and tried to take a pot shot at you."

My first feeling was one of indignation.

"Well, why in the hell didn't you tell me?"

"I wanted to see you sweat a little. You been gettin' a little cocky lately. I thought it was time to see if you could really go it alone."

"Why you . . ." I stuttered. But then a satisfying warmth rushed through me at the manner in which my sidekick had made certain that I would have maximum protection. I should have suspected that Joe would be around if it happened that I needed him.

Now that the tap was in on the Montmartre we sat back to await developments. They were slow in coming but Leeson called the pitch on what the eventual outcome would be.

"It's got to be Grant," he insisted one night as we cased a South Side warehouse. "I been thinking about that bastard a long time. Notice how he always seems to be wearin' a new suit? And those expensive ties?"

"You're just jealous of that good-lookin' moustache," I needled, not taking him too seriously.

A couple of days later we accidently encountered Grant and Seager, who had been working a job together. My car was in the garage and we were about to take a taxi down to Froelich's office.

"Say," Seager said innocently as Grant walked away from us to get cigarets. "You should see Grant's new buggy. It's a real beaut. Must have cost him a wad."

"What happened, Grant?" Leeson said curtly when Arnold returned. "You get prosperous all of a sudden?"

Grant looked uncomfortable. He muttered something to the effect that his wife had a rich aunt who had died and left them some money.

"How about that!" Leeson grated. "Hey, Paul, do you or Sam have a rich aunt who might drop dead conveniently?"

Seager's stony countenance reflected absolutely nothing. Nor did his tone as he told us he was knocking off for the day and walked away. Grant started to turn away, too, but Leeson stopped him.

"How about a lift down to the office in that new car?" Joe asked.

Grant displayed ill-concealed reluctance but finally agreed to drop us off.

Joe rode up front with him and I sat in the back as we started off. But we hadn't gone far when the sharp-eyed Leeson suddenly sat erect and barked at Grant:

"There's a loaded truck. Follow it!"

"Hey," protested Grant, "I'm going off now."

"The hell you are," Leeson retorted. "Follow that truck."

It seemed to me, even then, that Grant made an awkward job of it but I laid it to the manner in which Joe had rubbed him the wrong way. However, by the time Grant could turn the car around, once knocking off the engine and seemingly having trouble getting it started again, the truck was lost.

Leeson stared at him hard.

"Nice going," he spat at Grant. "I guess you earned your dough that time."

Grant glared back at Leeson.

"Just what the hell do you mean by that crack?" he blustered.

Leeson was ready for anything Grant wanted.

"I mean you lost that truck on purpose. And if you want to make something out of it, pull this jalopy over to the side."

Grant angrily shifted gears and drove us downtown without another word. As we got out and he pulled away, Leeson stood staring after him.

"I know that's the son of a bitch who's been selling us out," he growled.

"C'mon, Joe," I tugged at his arm. "You don't know any such damned thing. You just don't like the guy."

A few days later, I took a couple of days off to go see my folks in Galesburg, it having been a long time since my last visit. And there a series of events proved to me that Joe had a solid basis for his suspicions.

Still living in the house next door to that of my parents was a boyhood friend of mine who by this time had become a cashier in a Galesburg bank. Late that afternoon as he came home from work, we spotted each other and sat for about an hour on the porch talking about old times.

"Must be pretty exciting," he said longingly as I told him what I was doing.

"Well," I said, "it's a job. But I still take a drink now and then myself just to keep the halo from getting too tight and giving me a headache."

He laughed and I said, "By the way—and this is my day off so I'm not after information—but is there anywhere in town a man can get a bottle?"

"Sure," he told me. "You remember the Scanlon brothers we went to school with. Well, they got a pretty good garage business and they sell a little booze on the side. They'd let you have a bottle for old times' sake."

We talked of other things for a few minutes and then, looking puzzled, he told me that Joe, the eldest of the Scanlons, had been in the bank that very afternoon just before closing time at three o'clock.

"Seemed kind of upset," he mused. "And he made a whopping withdrawal. Five thousand bucks."

I dismissed it from my mind and went in to dinner. Then, later in the evening, I went to visit another old schoolmate of mine named Jimmy Griffin and was surprised when, in the course of his conversation, he, too, mentioned the Scanlons.

"Funny thing," he recalled, "I was in their office this afternoon. Had an appointment about some garage business. But while I was waiting in the reception room some fellow came in. I overheard him tell the switchboard girl that he was a special agent from Chicago and had important business with them. The girl talked to Joe Scanlon a few seconds and then told the guy to go right on in.

"A few minutes later, Joe came out in a helluva hurry and asked me to come back tomorrow because something unexpected had come up and he'd be too busy to talk to me. So I left."

My interest was piqued.

"What time was this?"

"Oh, shortly before three o'clock. I know, because my appointment with Joe Scanlon was for two-thirty and I had been waiting a couple of minutes when this fellow came in."

"What did this fellow who called himself an agent look like?" I asked casually.

"Well, he was a nice-looking guy. Well dressed. And, oh yes, he had one of those thin little movie-star moustaches."

Arnold Grant!

It all tied in perfectly; his visit and the timing of Joe Scanlon's sudden trip to the bank to make a five thousand dollar withdrawal. All of it together spelled shakedown.

Grant was really spreading out to work his way clear to Galesburg.

I knew that there would be, however, no means of proving my suspicion, no matter how neatly it meshed. The Scanlons had a perfect right to withdraw five thousand dollars from the bank and they would be certain to deny anything. But it strengthened my conviction that Leeson was right and that Grant was on the take. I'd better, I decided, report my findings to Froelich on my return to Chicago.

"When are you going back?" Jimmy Griffin asked me.

"Tomorrow."

"If it's all right with you," he said, "how about me riding back with you? I've got a girl friend in Chicago and I been thinking about going up for a few days."

I told him I'd be glad to have the company.

"You got room in your car for a few things?" he asked. "I been keeping in good with her family by taking some stuff up to them."

I grinned. The depression which had set in with the stock market crash in October of 1929 was getting steadily worse and Jimmy wasn't missing any bets when it came to putting himself in solid with the girl's family. I told him I had plenty of room for almost anything he wanted to take along.

The next day I drove around to his house to pick him up and he told me to sit and have a cup of coffee with his folks while he packed his gear in the rear of the car. I did and then, after a short while, he told me he was ready and we pulled out.

"You must have it pretty bad for this girl," I said, noting the bulky pile of articles stowed in the back of the car.

When we arrived in Chicago, Jimmy directed me to his girl friend's house and, being in a hurry, I helped him unpack his belongings while the girl's father appeared and started to carry various bundles into the house.

There were a couple of hams, some canned goods and, on the bottom, a large package which undoubtedly contained a half-dozen bottles of liquor. Hooking a finger in the wrapping, I tore it open and saw that I was right. Angrily, I spun on Jimmy.

"What the hell do you mean transporting alcohol in my car?"

Jimmy gave me a boyish grin.

"Don't be sore, Paul. I couldn't think of a safer way than in a government car with a government agent driving."

I had to laugh, shaking my head at his ingenuity and audacity.

"You take the cake," I told him. "But from now on you'd better get yourself another chauffeur."

The next morning, I reported in at Froelich's office and told him what I had learned in Galesburg and of my suspicions of Grant. But it was as I had known it would be. We needed more concrete evidence.

It wasn't long in coming and we got it from the tap on the Montmartre.

Most of the mob's protection payoffs were made by a hoodlum named Louie Volo at an auto parts store on South State Street which he used as a front to cover up his activities.

Chapman had been working the Montmartre tap shortly after my trip to Galesburg when there was a call for Ralph Capone. Chapman's record of the conversation made very interesting reading.

"Ralph? This Volo."

"Yeah?"

"That fed with the moustache is in here again."

"Again?"

"Yeah. He says he needs a grand pronto. What'll I do?"

"Put him on."

"Grant?"

"Yes."

"Look, enough is enough. Don't you think you're milkin' us a little too hard?"

"Well, I'm in a rather precarious position. And I have been a lot of help to you guys."

"Okay, okay. But enough's enough. You get too greedy, you son of a bitch, and we'll really pay you off. Now let me talk to Volo."

"Yeah, Ralph?"

"Give that greedy bastard a thousand. But you tell him that this is it for a long while, and that we expect a real good return on our investment—or else."

"Okay."

Underneath Chapman's transcription Lyle had written in his bold hand: "There's no question but that it was Grant on the phone!"

Leeson raged when Froelich showed the wire tap record of the conversation to us. Joe's big hands worked convulsively as he asked Froelich to let us bring Grant in and personally see that he was thrown in jail.

Froelich refused flatly.

"I'm afraid it's out of the question. In the first place, I'm not too sure this transcription would stand up in court. And, as in the case of Steelman, if this gets out that we have had a second defector it could ruin our growing reputation even more now than before."

There was only one way out, he insisted. He would confront Grant with all the evidence, including a deposition I made about the Galesburg incident, and Grant would be forced to resign quietly.

Which is the way it worked out.

CHAPTER 7

As a result of Grant's "resignation," the squad was brought up to full strength again with the addition of Bill Gardner. This, I thought as I met him in Froelich's office, was a good man.

Gardner was a superb physical specimen of about six feet, three inches with broad shoulders, an olive complexion, high cheek bones, jet-black hair and a way of looking right through you with his gleaming black eyes.

"You seem kind of familiar to me," I told him.

Froelich smiled.

"Gardner used to play football with the Carlisle Indians. An end, I believe. You probably have seen pictures of him."

Gardner was paired off with Friel at this time and, after they left to get Gardner settled in a hotel, Froelich told us that he had a special assignment for Leeson and me.

"Our reputation, the one we've tried so hard to protect, is about to start paying off," he said. "There's a fellow named Jack Martin, a runner for the mob, who contacted me at my hotel and offered to sell us information."

The mob ran itself as smoothly as any large business corporation. It had district offices all over town and every day each district office had to have a daily report at Guzik's office in the Wabash Hotel by 4:30 p.m. Martin was one of the men who picked up the reports in the various districts and delivered them to Guzik, the treasurer of the syndicate.

"Martin has a record as a petty thief," Froelich said. "He's been pulled in from time to time for looting hotel

89

rooms when he was a bell hop, rolling drunks and other minor infractions. But he's smart and puts up a good front, so the mob uses him. Here's his picture."

Froelich tossed us a police mug shot. Martin hadn't been at all abashed when it was taken, for it showed him smiling easily, disclosing an even set of teeth. He was a handsome devil with wide-spaced eyes and a firm chin. He wore his hair parted carefully in the middle.

"We're going to pay this guy one hundred dollars a week for information," Froelich disclosed. "Naturally, he can't home here. So I've set up the initial meeting for 5:30 p.m. today on the mezzanine of the Palmer House. It's usually crowded there at that time of day, so it should make good cover. You and he can set up whatever you want to do about future meetings but you'll have to arrange to meet him each week to make the payoff."

Martin, when I met him that afternoon at the Palmer House, was even better looking I noted than the police mug shot had indicated him to be. For a man who might be selling his life at a cheap figure, he seemed unconcerned with the possibility that he might be discovered in his doublecross of the mob.

"The way I set it up with the man," he said, referring to Froelich, "is that I'll manage to open the envelope whenever possible and get telephone numbers, confidential information, addresses, payoff figures and whatever else is available. These I'll pass along to you."

"All right," I agreed. "But you'd better be damned careful about contacting us."

He chuckled.

"I've got it all figured out. Run-of-the-mill stuff I'll just put in an envelope and mail to you. Uncle Sam, as I've got it figured, is the best bet. But if there's anything real hot, I'll have my sister bring it to you at your apartment."

I could visualize his sister. A mob trollop, I thought, with brassy blonde hair and wearing makeup an inch thick.

Never was I more mistaken in my life.

Because a few days later there was a knock at my

apartment door and, when I opened it, standing there was one of the most attractive women I'd ever seen.

"Mister Robsky?" she asked in a low, soothing voice.

"Yes."

I was curious, for I didn't connect a woman of her class with Jack Martin.

"I'm Mavis Martin. My brother asked me to bring you an envelope."

I invited her inside and, as she entered, inspected her with careful appreciation. Mavis Martin, I observed clinically, was about five feet, two inches tall and had the tiniest feet and the shapeliest legs I'd seen in a long time. Her russet hair curled naturally around her forehead and at the nape of her neck, and her skin was translucently clear, clean and glowing. She was a strikingly beautiful woman and I judged her to be about twenty-five years old.

"Here's the envelope," she said, refusing a chair. "I'm sorry, but I can't stay."

There was the merest hint of disapproval in her tone and the wide brown eyes with their golden specks looked at me as if I was some species of insect.

"Do you know what this is?" I asked her.

"No," she replied, still standing. "But having occasionally met some of my brother's acquaintances and 'business associates,' I can well imagine."

"Now wait a minute," I protested, for suddenly it had become important to me that I should be elevated a few notches in her estimation and I was certain that a woman of her charm and apparent good breeding wouldn't sell her brother down the river. "I'd like you to understand what this is all about."

"I don't want to understand," she said in that low, musical voice. "I know something about what Jack does and, if I had my way, he'd get himself a decent job and not associate with your type."

She started for the door again but I couldn't let her go like this.

"It isn't what you think," I stopped her by grasping one firm, warm arm.

She flinched but then I could feel her relax slowly as I added quickly:

"I'm a federal agent. Your brother, Jack, is doing us an invaluable service."

Mavis Martin drew a deep breath of surprise and the brown eyes opened wide.

"You mean . . . ?"

"Yes," I nodded. "Look, I was about to have a cup of coffee. Sit down and I'll tell you about it."

She hesitated momentarily and then shrugged out of her coat at my continued insistence and sat down guardedly. A knitted suit molded itself to her body and the curves were all of the right proportion and in the proper places.

Over coffee, I explained to her about her brother's deal with Froelich and how I was to be his contact man. At last she interrupted me.

"But won't this put him in great danger?"

"Yes," I told her honestly, "but we'll keep our ear to the ground and do our best to protect him."

She nodded and then gave me a gleaming white smile, her golden-brown eyes holding a new light of friendly interest.

"It's dangerous for you, too, I imagine."

"Interesting and exciting is the way I like to think about it."

"That gives me an idea, Mister Robsky . . ."

"Paul," I suggested.

"All right, Paul," she continued. "It so happens that I am a free-lance writer, magazine articles and things like that. Why couldn't I do a magazine article on you and your group?"

I couldn't help but laugh out loud.

"That's the last thing we want, publicity," I grinned. "While we are pretty well pegged by the mob, the less they or anybody else knows about us, the better we like it. No, I don't think that the boss would go for anything like that.

But," I seized the opportunity, "as long as I've cost you a magazine fee, the least I can do is to take you to dinner some time. Like, say, tonight, for a starter."

Mavis gave me that dazzling smile again, her eyes crinkling at the corners. The musical quality of her voice fascinated me.

"You're a rapid worker, Paul. But I'm so happy that Jack is doing something worthwhile for a change that the least I can do to show my appreciation is to have dinner with you."

We had dinner that night at a tiny Italian restaurant. Mavis was radiant in a low-cut gown and, in the soft gleam of the candlelight, I could see that this, for sure, was all woman. And over dinner she told me how she and Jack had come to Chicago from their Iowa farm home after the death of their parents.

"Jack has been in and out of trouble constantly," she sighed. "I guess, being at loose ends and times being what they are, he just fell in with the wrong people. I was lucky. I had taken a journalism course at the University of Iowa and I managed to get a job on the Tribune. For the past year, though, I have been doing free-lance magazine work. But I do worry a great deal about Jack and really appreciate what you are doing for him."

I couldn't take much credit for myself in that department, I thought to myself. Her brother very well could wind up suddenly dead if the mob found out what he was doing.

After dinner we drove out along Lake Michigan and, finding a secluded spot, sat and talked quietly as several hours sped past. And I found Mavis to be a sincere and sensitive woman as well as a sprightly conversationalist.

"Gracious," she said suddenly, "I hadn't realized it was so late. We'd better go now, Paul."

Her brother, Jack, I knew, had a room in the free-wheeling Liberty Hotel. Mavis lived, however, in a neat, orderly apartment house in Jackson Park. As I left her at her door, she said, "I hope we can make it again soon, Paul."

"I do, too," I told her. "But my hours are kind of irregular and I work a good many nights."

"Well, I don't have any permanent attachments," she said encouragingly. "I'm usually at home in the evenings."

Impulsively she reached up and kissed me on the cheek.

"Thanks for a really lovely evening."

I was whistling as I walked to the car. Chicago had been a fairly lonesome city for me on the occasions I had been off duty. It promised to be somewhat more interesting now.

It was. For, while Jack Martin sent in most of his information by mail, on the average of once every two weeks he would send Mavis to me with something hot which he had discovered: the imminent arrival of a big shipment of whiskey from Canada, word of a suddenly called meeting of the mob's big shots, and the information that "Snorky," as the syndicate referred to Al Capone, was on his way back to Chicago after finishing his jail term in Philadelphia.

"I'm worried about you, Paul," Mavis told me one night when we returned to her cozy apartment after another dinner date. "Jack says things are really likely to break loose once Capone gets back to the city. He's sure that they'll try to make reprisals against your squad."

I pulled her down and she cuddled on my lap, her head on my shoulder and her soft lips against my ear.

"Please be careful."

I kissed her.

"Don't you worry, honey. I'm always careful."

Almost two weeks passed before I saw Mavis again. Acting on information from her brother, we had staged a whirlwind roundup which netted two breweries, two large liquor drops and a half dozen speakeasies. I was still in bed when she came to my apartment one morning and I knew she was agitated from the manner in which she clung to me when I kissed her.

"What's the matter, honey?" I asked.

Her voice was tight.

"Capone's back. And Jack says to tell you that there's a big meeting of all the top men in the mob somewhere tonight. He doesn't know where, but his information is that your squad is supposed to be the number one item of business."

I grinned at her, although I had a peculiarly hollow feeling in the pit of my stomach.

"How about making some coffee while I take a shower?" I asked her. "And don't worry about us. We can take care of ourselves."

Later I picked up Leeson and we went down town and told Froelich about Martin's tip. The usually matter-of-fact Froelich became grim. It was clear that he was worried, too.

"There's no telling what to expect, but we'll have to walk very carefully," he said.

"Hell," Joe grunted, "we knew he'd be back sooner or later."

We had cause to wish it was much, much later within a few days when it was brought home to us with force that Capone had unwrapped his brass knuckles.

It started with an anonymous telephone tip, which wasn't unusual. A great many of them were phonies but we made a practice of checking them all out carefully.

This one, from a woman who refused to give her name, provided the address of a garage in the South Side warehouse district where, our nameless informant insisted, there was a brewery in operation.

Joe and I, believing we were unobserved, began a watch on it and had seen several trucks enter. We kept it under surveillance for several nights and Joe, usually a calm man despite his explosive temper, on this particular night seemed peculiarly edgy.

"I don't like it," he said suddenly.

"Why not?"

"Well, every night now we've seen trucks going in there. But, you know something, we haven't seen any of them come out."

"Maybe they move them later," I suggested.

"Maybe," he muttered. "But I still don't like it."

At this moment, another truck rumbled down the street and turned into the garage, the doors swinging closed behind it.

Joe's suspicions had their effect on me and, while we were busy watching the garage, I had an uneasy feeling. Perhaps it is the result of living this kind of a life, of sharpening the instincts of a hunted animal, but I happened to look into the rear-view mirror and in the light from the corner street lamp I saw a black touring car with side curtains speeding toward us. The first thing that hit me was that it was being driven without its headlights on.

"Hit the floor," I barked at Joe.

In one lightning motion and without question Leeson flipped the handle of the car door and tumbled out head first to the sidewalk. I dove out right behind him, tearing one knee out of my trousers, as the thunder of two submachineguns chattered through the stillness of the night. The glass windows in our car were smashed out as with the stroke of a giant hammer and bullets ripped into the tonneau. I heard a tire let go and then the angry sounds of the bullets chewing into the radiator of our car as the car swept past. Flat on the sidewalk, Joe and I fired at the disappearing target without any sign of scoring a hit.

"Close," Joe growled icily as he got to his feet apparently unperturbed.

My knees wanted to quiver but I was as mad as hell.

"Let's go shake down that garage."

We sprinted across the street and, finding the doors locked as we expected, shot into the lock and pushed our way inside.

The building was completely empty. Not only that, but it clearly had been standing idle for quite a while considering the dust and accumulated rubbish.

"We were decoyed," Joe grated, pointing to a pair of doors in the rear. "They drove in the front and right out the back. They were setting us up for their little party. It's a damned good thing for us that you happened to see them coming."

We walked back to our car and stood there silently, surveying it ruefully. Every window had been shot out. The side was pock marked with bullet holes which continued along the hood and had mangled the front of the radiator. The more I looked, the madder I got.

"What a mess," I said and then, feeling a cold air on my knee, added angrily, "Not only that, but they ruined one of my best suits."

"You could have come up with some worse holes than that," Joe grinned suddenly. "I guess we were kind of lucky at that."

Reaching down, I tore off the dangling patch of cloth and then put on a raincoat which I kept in the rear of the car to cover the hole. As I put it on, I noticed that there were two bullet holes in one of the sleeves.

"Look," I joked to keep from shaking, "I'm a sieve."

We walked until we came to an all-night restaurant and Joe called our constantly manned office in the Transportation Building to have a tow truck pick up our well-ventilated car. Then we called a cab and, after dropping Leeson off, I started home. Suddenly I changed my mind, although it was after two o'clock in the morning, and decided that I'd drop by and tell Mavis that I wanted her brother to try to find out who worked the choppers on us.

It was apparent, when she answered the door, that she had been asleep. But, I thought, I'd never seen her looking more exquisite. The smooth cheeks were flushed with sleep and the tousled spray of her red-gold hair was enchanting. She had thrown on a shimmering negligee and was a picture of utter loveliness.

"Paul, what is it?" she asked in alarm, grasping my arm and drawing me inside. "Is something wrong?"

"Hold on now," I chuckled. "Take it easy. If I had known I was going to upset you, I wouldn't have dropped in. But we had a little shooting scrape tonight and I wanted you to get in touch with Jack the first thing tomorrow and tell him to see if he can find out who was gunning for us."

"Your coat," she interrupted, pointing to the bullet holes in the sleeve. "Are you hurt?"

I reassured her that I was all right.

"The only thing wrong with me is a ruined pair of trousers and a skinned knee."

She insisted on taking my coat and fixing me a cup of coffee and I leaned back thankfully on the couch as she fussed around me while I told her what had happened. Her nearness and her fragrance was very disturbing and, after I finished my coffee, I told her I'd better be leaving.

"Nonsense," she insisted. "You'll sleep right there on the couch. It's too late to be going home."

With swift efficiency, she made up a bed for me.

"Now you get in bed and I'll come back and tuck you in," she smiled.

I stretched out wearily. The only light in the room was one on an end table beside the couch when she reappeared. Mavis bent over me solicitously and, as she kissed me goodnight, her negligee parted. My arms went up around her and tenderly I pulled her down beside me. She came willingly, even eagerly.

I freed one hand and switched off the light.

Sunlight was streaming in the windows when I awakened. Mavis was gone and the door to her bedroom was closed. However, I must have been awakened by the sounds of movement within her bedroom for within a few minutes the door opened and she appeared fully dressed.

"Good morning," I said.

She looked at me and blushed. "Good morning, Paul."

"Mavis, about last night . . ." I said haltingly.

Swiftly she was beside me, bending down and closing my mouth with a soft kiss.

"Don't worry about it, honey," she murmured with a tender frankness. "It was what we both wanted."

Then, tousling my hair, she told me to shower while she made breakfast.

Later, as I held her close to me just before leaving, she whispered in my ear:

"Always remember one thing as far as I'm concerned,

Paul. You're the best man I've ever known. In bed or out."

Her face flamed and I laughed delightedly.

"I wonder what old man Austin would say to that?"

Her eyebrows arched inquisitively.

"Who's 'old man Austin' and what did he say?"

I grinned down at her.

"Maybe I'll tell you about it some time. But now I've got to get going."

As I walked down the street, feeling that I'd risk getting shot at any night in the week for some one like Mavis, I thought again of that day shortly after my assignment to Greenville when I had been riding through the countryside with my old boss, Austin, and we passed a field in which stood a handsome, red-coated bull.

Solemnly, Austin had tipped his hat.

"Why did you do that?" I blurted.

"Mr. Robsky," Austin replied austerely, "that there is a prize bull."

I had nodded, still uncomprehending.

"And, Mr. Robsky," Austin had said with complete imperturbability, "that there bull is the only one I know around here that's built better than me."

To each his own, I thought now, and went whistling on my way.

CHAPTER 8

Unfortunately for our hopes, Jack Martin wasn't able to come up with the slightest lead on the identity of the killers who shot up our car and we never did get a clue as to who they were.

But, through Mavis, he did put us in touch with one of the most weird creatures I encountered during our entire tenure in Chicago.

"Jack said to tell you that there is a woman named Sarah Hanks who must be the most brazen person in the whole world," Mavis told me. "Imagine, she's been shaking down the mob."

Sarah Hanks, as it developed, was indeed making the mob pay off on the threat of going to the police. And she had backed the mob into a corner by informing them in no uncertain terms that, as well as being related to a highly placed Chicago politician, she also had a carefully prepared list of their operations, constantly kept up to date. This, she threatened, would be mailed immediately to Chicago's crime-busting organization of business leaders known as the "Secret Six" as well as to high federal authorities and the newspapers if anything suspicious happened to her.

"Jack says that he thinks she'd be willing to play it two ways from the jack, whatever that means," Mavis reported.

"He means," I told her, "that he believes she'd be willing to take their money and sell us information, too."

Mavis' brother had sent us this Sarah Hanks' address and Leeson and I found it to be an ancient but carefully

tended house on the North Side. There was an old-fashioned bell pull in the door, a portal decorated with leaded
panes of colored glass reminiscent of the Gay Nineties. I
tugged on the bell pull and there was a jangling sound from
the rear of the house.

Almost immediately the door opened and both of us
stared unbelievingly. Confronting us, arms akimbo, was a
slatternly woman in her late fifties with a hatchet face and
deep-set eyes like two holes burned in a bedsheet. Stringy
hair wriggled down from under a dust cap like wisps of
straw and she had the complexion of a slightly used piece
of sandpaper. Around her neck hung more beads that I'd
even seen on one person, possibly six or eight strands,
dangling down over what once had been an evening gown
which had been cut off raggedly just below the knees.
Completing this implausible costume was a pair of man's
shoes.

The voice matched the outfit. It was stridently shrill,
announcing to a dumfounded world that this was a person
accustomed to neither nonsense nor interference.

"Yes? What is it you want?"

I found my tongue first, to my utter discomfort.

"Mrs. Shanks?"

"The name, young man, is Hanks."

The blood crept up into my face and I stuttered.

"I beg your pardon, ma'am. I meant, uh, Hanks. Uh,
we thought, that is, I mean . . ."

Leeson, muffling a grin, came to the rescue.

"Mrs. Hanks, we're prohibition agents and we'd like to
talk to you."

"Well, come in, come in," she snapped in that reedy
voice. "I don't know what you want with me but come in
and get it said."

We shuffled inside and she led us into a dim parlor
which matched the facade of this gingerbread house of
another era. The furniture was all outmoded and yet, I
noted, it was clean and in good repair. Standing on a huge
mahogany sideboard were the pictures of three pretty girls

in various stages of their teens. The woman observed me
looking at them.

"My girls a few years ago," she volunteered. "They're
away now. I wouldn't want them in this God-forsaken
city. Now, what is it you wanted?"

I had, by this time, recovered my shattered composure.

"We have reason to believe that you might be able to
help us," I told her. "Contrary to public opinion, the Prohibition Bureau is trying to dry up Chicago and . . ."

"What's your name, sonny?" she interrupted.

Confusion set in on me again.

"Uh, sorry, I'm Paul Robsky and this is my partner
Joe Leeson."

"Yes," she snapped, "I've heard talk that you've finally
gotten off your butts."

"Well," I continued, "as I said . . ."

"I know, sonny," she shrilled. "I know. Some loud
mouth has told you that I know something about what's
going on around here and you think maybe I'll provide
some free information."

"Not free," I managed to insert. "We . . ."

"That's all right then," she stopped me again. "Sit
down."

We sat down.

"Now," she continued, hiking up the sawed off dress so
it disclosed both bony knees, "I am in position to provide
you with information but, as you said, for a price. What's
it worth?"

I hesitated, partially because I was confused by this
amazing woman. She thought I was hedging.

"What I know was worth five hundred bucks to Attili
Agramonti to keep it quiet," she cackled. "So it ought to
be worth the same amount to you to find out about it."

I told her that if we considered it a good haul it probably would be worth that much to the government.

"Hah!" she screeched derisively. "I'll bet one place
know about has over fifty grand worth of booze stashe
away. You knock over this one spot and if it ain't wort

hat much then you keep your five hundred, and also keep the hell away from here in the future."

We agreed that it was a deal and Mrs. Hanks promptly gave us an address on South Wells Street. The liquor was in a large garage, she said, which was owned by an elderly Pole named Stanley Zibak.

"Old Zibak is a square shooter," she said. "He didn't want to rent the place to Agramonti but him and a couple of his gorillas 'persuaded' Zibak he'd be healthier this way."

As we prepared to leave, I asked Mrs. Hanks if she wasn't afraid that Agramonti and his muscle might find out about her selling them out and pay her a visit.

"Sonny," she said, "I ain't been afraid of nobody ever in my life. Besides, who's gonna tell him, you?"

I shook my head.

"No ma'am. Not me."

Then I did it again.

"Goodbye, Mrs. Shanks."

It seemed to me that sparks shot out of her eyes.

"Hanks, damn you. Hanks," she almost shouted, and then slammed the door so hard I thought all that fancy colored glass was going to fall out.

Leeson was laughing so hard he almost doubled over.

"Dammit," I grunted. "I just couldn't help it. She sure looks like a Shanks to me, the damned old harridan."

And "Shanks" she remained to all of us from that time on.

We lost no time in staking out the garage at the address she had given us. It was padlocked during the daytime, a check revealed, but we wanted more than the liquor it contained. We wanted Agramonti, a mobster with a reputation for viciousness who had a long record of arrests and no convictions.

Adjoining the garage was a tiny house in which, we discovered, the elderly Zibak, a spare, stoop-shouldered man with iron-gray hair, lived quietly with his wife. They retired early each night and when, on the second night of our watch, a touring car and a truck entered the garage there was no sign of movement within the Zibak house.

"Probably scared to death of those hoods and don't know what to do about them," Leeson sympathized.

There was an every-other-night pattern to the visits which Agramonti and his men made to the Zibak garage and the answer was obvious. This was one of the mob's principal storage spots for its top-grade imported whiskey and it was moved from here, on clock-like schedule, to the various cutting and rebottling plants.

As had become customary, we set up our raid so that we would strike simultaneously from front, rear and roof. This being our find, Leeson and I had the privilege of driving our truck through the double doors in front. The raid was set up for 2 a.m. as Agramonti's entourage usually arrived at about 1:30.

Joe and I were parked several blocks away on an intersecting street as the time neared the morning we picked to make the raid and, like clockwork, we saw Agramonti's touring car leading the truck past the intersection. Hurrying to the corner, I saw them turn into the garage and the doors close. At two minutes of two, Joe started the motor and put the truck into gear. I wedged myself into a corner of the seat and took a firm grip on the tommygun I carried.

The truck lunged forward, gathered momentum and wheeled smoothly into South Wells Street. Then we were bearing down on the garage and, without slowing, Joe spun the wheel and aimed the nose of the truck at those doors. They burst apart as if made of cheesecake and before Joe could bring our truck to a halt we plowed head on into the mobsters' truck, which had been backed in and bashed in the whole front of it.

Three men who had been loading the truck were scattered like tenpins. Two of them rose slowly and raised their hands as they looked into my tommygun. The other one lay there with blood oozing from a cut on his head where he had struck a steel upright.

A quick look showed me more whiskey, the cases stacked in orderly tiers, than I had ever seen before in one spot. Then I caught a movement out of the side of my eye and saw a small, glass-enclosed office along one wall. What I had noticed even as my eyes slowly became accustomed to the glare of the garage, was the light being doused in the office. It was relatively dark in there but I knew someone was hiding in the cubicle.

"Come out of there," I called as I saw others of the squad just entering the back door down the long length of the garage. "This is a federal raid."

Their answer was a burst of gunfire which splattered into some cases of whiskey behind us. Joe and I hit the deck, as did our two standing prisoners. Springing into a crouch, I cut loose with a long, hammering burst from the tommygun, spraying the tiny office thoroughly. The glass dropped out of every window and there was a scream of pain as one hoodlum jerked upright, took a few staggering steps through the swinging door leading from the office and pitched on his face.

"There's at least one more in there," Leeson yelled. "Watch out for the son of a bitch."

I knew that, from their original fusillade of pistol shots, so I moved forward cautiously, my finger on the trigger, ready to cut loose instantly with another burst. But there wasn't a sound from inside. Joe moved up beside me as I booted open the door and pushed the tommygun through ahead of me.

There wasn't anybody in the office.

"What the hell?" Joe said in a puzzled voice.

It was a tiny room with a battered desk against the wall, two rickety chairs and a marred metal filing cabinet which later proved to be empty. Two glasses, partially filled with whiskey, still sat on the desk. The bottle had toppled to the floor and smashed on the concrete.

Joe pointed to the glasses.

"There were two of them in here. But where in hell did the other guy get to?"

There weren't any stairs leading up to the roof and there apparently was no other door out of the little office.

"Damned if I know . . ." I started to reply, and then

my eyes centered on the floor where the bottle of whiskey had smashed.

Beside the pool of liquor, and facing right to the wall, was the wet imprint of a man's shoe.

The lower half of the wall had been panelled in wood at some long previous date. At the spot where I noticed the alcoholic imprint of the shoe, a large commercial calendar, displaying the tinted charms of a nude woman reclining on a divan, covered a large section of the upper wall.

"Whoever it was, he probably admired that 'art,' " I said to Joe as I moved over to the wall, "but I doubt like hell if he did it in the dark while standing in a whiskey footbath."

Sharply I rapped the wall with the muzzle of the tommygun. There was a hollow echo and I ripped down the calendar to disclose a concealed doorway which fitted into the wooden wainscot so perfectly as to be practically invisible. The bottom edge of the calendar had hidden a small fingerhole which could be used to open the door.

"Stand back," I rapped at Joe, thinking it might be a closet and that our missing man might be inside ready to blast away.

But when I pulled the door open there, stretched in front of us, was a dark passageway.

"We're really smart," I growled disgustedly. "We cover the front, the back and the roof, and we overlook the fact that this probably connects with Zibak's house right next door."

"Let's go," Leeson shot back and, producing a flashlight, plunged into the corridor with me on his heels.

It did, as we suspected, lead directly into the Zibak house for it brought us out in the kitchen. And, as we burst in, the old man appeared in the doorway to another room and turned on the kitchen light. He was almost in a panic.

"What is it?" he asked in a trembling flow of words. "I hear much noise in the garage. My wife goes for drink of water here in kitchen. Man runs through house and knocks her down. Now you come."

"Where's the man?" Leeson demanded.

"He go out side door," Zibak said as, hands shaking, he almost ignored us and began to run a glass of water from the tap. "I must get drink for Mama."

"Where's your wife?" Joe asked.

"In parlor on floor," Zibak beckoned us to follow him as he carried the glass of water through a small dining room and under a tassel-decorated arch into a sparsely furnished living room.

A stout, white-haired woman lay on a well-worn carpet. Close by was a doorway which led to a side porch on the other side from the garage. The woman was moaning. Her eyes fluttered and her face was as white as the spotless linen cloth on the dining-room table.

"What is? What is?" she quavered in an almost indistinguishable voice.

"Quiet, Mama," old Zibak patted her shoulder tenderly.

"Let's get her up on the couch," big, rough Joe Leeson said compassionately. With that he picked her up as if she had been a child and lowered her gently onto an overstuffed sofa.

Zibak knelt beside her and, while Joe raised her head, tried to give her some water. It ran down her chin onto her flannel bathrobe. Vacant-eyed, the woman rolled her head from side to side.

"Take it easy, ma'am," Joe told her softly. "It's gonna be all right. Just take it easy." Then, in an aside to Zibak, he directed: "Listen, Pop, you'd better get a doctor. I don't like the way she looks."

Mrs. Zibak's eyes were closed now and she was breathing in shallow, spasmodic bursts. Joe took out a handkerchief, wet it with some of the water from the glass and began to bathe her forehead. I rubbed her wrists as the old man went to the sideboard and fumbled with the telephone.

There was a noise from the kitchen and we looked up as Chapman came into the room.

"Ssssh!" Joe whispered.

Chapman walked over silently, looked at us and then motioned that he was going back to the garage. We nodded and I told him in an undertone that we'd be along soon. But it was more than a half hour later before the doctor arrived and we walked back into the kitchen with Zibak trailing us disconsolately.

"Mama not been well," he said.

"Take it easy old-timer," Joe said. "We'll be in the garage and, while we have to talk to you, it'll keep 'til the doctor gets your missus taken care of."

"I be over," Zibak said gratefully.

We went back and saw that the other boys had tidied up the job in the garage. Old Mrs. "Shanks" had really delivered because Chapman, who was making the inventory, estimated cautiously that we had confiscated at least $75,000 worth of imported whiskies and other liquors.

The main items were four hundred cases of bonded whiskey, five hundred one-gallon jugs of top-grade bourbon and assorted cases of champagne, cordials and liqueurs. We also had three prisoners, one with a very sore head, and one corpse who turned out to be a much-wanted triggerman named Ziggy Laterno.

But the biggest fish, Attilio Agramonti, had escaped the net. None of the prisoners would identify him but we knew from "Shanks' " tip-off that he was the boss of this operation.

Joe and I were appreciatively sampling one of the bottles of imported scotch when old man Zibak finally appeared. He told us that his wife was asleep and that his daughter, who lived nearby, had arrived at his summons to stay with her. He looked shaky so we slipped him a stiff drink.

"I know what they do here is wrong," he confessed. "But the man who comes to rent garage gives no chance. He says he rent. I say no, not break American laws. He hold gun up and say he rent. So he rent."

"Could you identify him for us?" I asked.

"No know him," Zibak shook his head.

"How about if I show you a picture?" I suggested,

thinking of the mug shot of Agramonti we had obtained after Sarah "Shanks' " tip-off.

"No know him," Zibak reiterated stubbornly. "I think I not even know him from picture. I think I don't want Mama hurt no matter what happen to everything else."

It was that simple. No matter what we might have threatened, Zibak knew he had a better chance refusing the law than he had defying the deadly Agramonti.

"He don't know anything. He just rented the building," Leeson said defensively to Chapman. Then he turned to Zibak, pressed one of our cards into his hand and told him: "Go on home, old-timer. You got enough trouble. If you think of anything, give us a call."

Feet dragging and head down, Zibak walked off slowly.

Two days later Joe and I were getting ready to visit "Shanks" and pay her the five hundred dollars she had coming when we received a call from Zibak's daughter. She said her father wanted to see us.

"How's your mother?" I asked her.

Her voice was muffled. "She died yesterday. The doctor said it was a heart attack."

Joe and I felt like intruders when we drove up to the Zibak house. A small wreath with a black ribbon hung on the front door and we sat in the car a few moments staring at it, feeling almost as if we had contributed to Mrs. Zibak's death. As we got out of the car, the door opened and old Zibak came to meet us, puffing on a hand-carved meerschaum pipe.

"We're sorry, Mr. Zibak," Joe said.

"Is not your fault. You good man. Mama not being well long time. Is man who knock her down who kill her. Is gangster Agramonti."

We were speechless for a moment.

"But," I exclaimed, "I thought you told us you couldn't identify the man who rented your place."

The old man drew himself up straight and there was a simple dignity in his mien.

"That before he kill Mama," he said. "Now I no have to worry about Mama no more. For me I not afraid."

He would, he told us, be glad to identify Agramonti as the man who rented his garage and as the one who escaped through his house the night of our raid. Our next step was to put Agramonti under arrest but finding him was something else again.

Mavis and I had a date that night and I asked her to contact her brother, Jack, and see if he could find out for us where Agramonti hung out. Shortly thereafter I received a plain post card at my apartment. All it said was "Allen's Pool Hall, South Clark Street."

"I understand it's a pretty tough joint," I told Joe as we drove to Allen's the next afternoon. Joe merely grunted.

We paused inside the front door to take stock of the situation. There were a half dozen young punks shooting pool, all of them from their dress and manner obvious gangland recruits biding their time on the fringe of underworld acceptance. One of them, a pasty-faced youth with oiled black hair and a cigaret dangling contemptuously from slack lips, made it clear that he was the house man as he sauntered over to us.

"Whatcha want?"

"Where's Attilio?" Joe asked quietly.

"Who wantsa know?"

"I do," Joe said, an edge creeping into his voice.

"You look like a dick," the young punk sneered. "Why dontcha get lost?"

Joe's hand moved like a striking snake, gathering a handful of the youth's shirt and yanking him up on tiptoe until their faces were only an inch apart. The force of Joe's movement snapped the cigaret right out of the hoodlum's mouth. Joe's tone was ice cold.

"Listen, sonny boy, you'd better be a good little fellow or I'll knock your ass off. Now, I'm gonna ask you one more time, real nice, where's Agramonti?"

The house man's face had turned a sickly green and, his bravado completely gone, he jerked his head toward the rear. He could hardly talk.

"In the back room."

"Thanks," Joe grinned, letting him go. "Now stay the hell out of the way and you won't get yourself hurt."

We walked back and Leeson lifted one of those size twelve feet and kicked the door open. Inside, sitting at a table talking to a companion, was Agramonti, a tall, stiletto-thin man with the lined face of a Mephistopheles. He and the other, a bull-chested man with hair curling out over the collar of his silk shirt, had their coats off. Agramonti wore a gun in the shoulder holster he hadn't even bothered to take off. We stared at each other for several long seconds and Agramonti's hand began to move toward his gun.

"Go ahead," Leeson taunted him. "Go for it."

Agramonti did. But the ready Leeson launched himself head first over the table and drove Agramonti over backwards. The other man fell off his chair, started drawing a knife as he came up and I eliminated him by bringing the fisted butt of my .38 down on top of his head.

Agramonti never had a chance. Leeson slapped the gun out of his hand, hoisted him to his feet and doubled him over with a wallop to the stomach.

"That's for Mrs. Zibak," he grunted. Then he straightened the mobster up with a roundhouse right flush on the nose which brought a rush of blood and rocketed Agramonti flat on his back.

"And that one," Joe growled as he dusted off his hands, "was just for the hell of it."

We surveyed our two recumbent opponents and Joe grinned:

"It didn't take you long to get rid of that one."

"Economy of motion," I told him. "I'm the dainty type."

When we hauled them outside, the pool room was empty. We took them down and booked them on every charge we could think up and the desk sergeant, looking at Agramonti's swollen nose, asked what had happened to him.

"He slipped on a banana peel," Joe chuckled.

It was one of the misfortunes of the era in Chicago that

it was easier to get out of jail than it was to get in. And we were concerned for old Zibak when we heard that Agramonti quickly was released on bail. Joe and I made a special visit to him to try to get him to move in with his daughter, but he refused. The only other recourse was to get Froelich to intercede with high police officials and make certain that an order went down to the local precinct to maintain a special watch on the old man. We felt better when we checked up and found that the order had been given.

But there was no accounting for the almost maniacal manner in which the mob ruled Chicago, nor for the cheapness in which the underworld held human life.

Three days later, we received another call from Zibak's daughter. She was beside herself with anxiety.

"My father has been coming here for all his meals," she wept. "He didn't come last night and he hasn't been here all day today. I went over to his house but he's not there. I'm worried sick."

Leeson and I drove immediately to the old man's house. There was, as she had said, no sign of her father.

Except that in the back yard we found the carved meerschaum pipe with the stem bitten clean through.

And under a rose bush where it had been tossed was an axe with what a laboratory examination proved to be human hair and blood on the blade. The hair was iron gray.

No trace ever was to be found of Zibak's body. But it was obvious that gangland vengeance had been swift and violent.

It preyed relentlessly on both our minds. Joe and I spent two days drinking in my apartment and then, returning to duty, were bleary-eyed and haggard when we went to make a payoff to Mrs. Hanks for another profitable tip she had telephoned in while we were busy on the Zibak case.

"You two look terrible," she cackled, and I thought grimly about the pot calling the kettle black. "What you need is a drink; a good drink."

She poured us a drink in the kitchen and I found myself telling her all the details of the Zibak affair and how
we were certain that we never would be able to prove our
suspicions that Agramonti had killed the old man. For
once she was quiet as she listened. Then her shrill voice
erupted.

"That son of a bitch. I'll get him for you."

We asked her how she figured to do that.

"Easy," she snapped. "I'll get word to him that I got
hot information to sell; something he'd damned well better buy if he wants to keep me quiet. He'll come and,
well, you two had better be here when I start yelling."

She called us two days later and told us that Agramonti
would be at her house at nine o'clock that night. We were
there two hours earlier, just to be certain that we were
unobserved, and waited anxiously in a bedroom just off
the old-fashioned parlor with the shades drawn and the
door cracked. We thought we had missed the boat as nine
o'clock passed but, at nine-thirty, the doorbell clanged
and we heard Agramonti strut into the parlor. He didn't
waste any time.

"What you got to sell, old woman? I'm in a hurry and
ain't got no time to waste."

"Shanks," was a great actress.

"You'd better listen to this and be prepared to pay
a good price," she shrilled in that cracked falsetto. "I saw
you do it."

"Do what?"

"I saw you knock off old man Zibak."

There was a long pause. Then Agramonti's tone was ·
deadly.

"How could you see me? It was dark as hell."

"I saw you all right. I was hiding in the rose bushes
right where you threw the axe."

There was another silence and once again Agramonti's
venomous voice broke the stillness.

"Okay, so you saw me. Okay, so I did it. Now, what's
to keep me from knockin' off an old broad like you, too?"

"Shanks" laughed shrilly.

"I got it all wrote down in a sworn affidavit. That and how I'm gettin' you to pay off. So, if anything happens to me, the right people will get it all."

"Awright, so how do I know you won't keep right on bleedin' me?"

"You don't, honey," Mrs. Hanks said, then, raising her voice, called to us: "All right, boys, come take this pigeon away."

We bolted into the room but we hadn't counted on Agramonti's resourcefulness. He stepped behind "Shanks," wrapped one long arm around her wrinkled neck to hold her in front of him and covered us with his gun. We had separated as we entered the room and Agramonti, holding us at bay, backed to the front door, spun "Shanks" toward us and closed the front door behind him as he fled.

We raced out the door after him and received quite a shock. The fleeing mobster had knocked a porch rocker over in front of the door and Leeson and I took a header right over it and down the front steps. By the time we pulled ourselves together and regained our feet rather groggily, his car was roaring down the street and turning the corner.

Mrs. Hanks was on the porch screeching at us.

"He lives in the Courtland Hotel, room 710. That's where I got in touch with him."

It was our best bet and we sprinted around the block to where we had parked our car and sped to the Courtland. The small lobby was plush and empty, except for an attendant reading a magazine at the switchboard behind the desk.

"Agramonti in?" Leeson demanded.

"Yeah," the clerk said. "Just went up."

We fretted at the elevator as it descended in answer to our ring, and then told the boy who was running it to take us to the seventh floor. On his direction, we headed for room 710 and, pausing outside the door, heard a thumping noise from within. We each stood to one side and Leeson reached over and hammered on the panel.

"Come on out, Agramonti, or we're coming in after you."

Two shots from inside splintered the panel. Then after a short, wary silence Joe shot into the lock and kicked the door to open it but it was held by a chain on the inside. Leeson drew back and flung himself against it, snapping the chain and hurling himself flat on the floor inside the darkened room.

I reached around the edge of the door, felt for the light switch and turned on the lights. Agramonti was nowhere to be seen. Then we saw a strip of bedsheet fastened to the steam radiator at one of the open windows. But there was no weight on it for it fluttered in the breeze.

"There he is," Joe said, pointing downward.

Agramonti lay spreadeagled on a third floor stone terrace, obviously dead.

The sheet dangled far short of a smaller fifth floor terrace which he apparently had been trying to reach. But he had either mis-timed his swing or lost his grip and fallen, striking the fifth floor parapet and hurtling two floors farther down.

"He got away from us," Joe said, "but he couldn't get away from what he had coming."

We drove back later to tell Mrs. Hanks what had happened. Then, as we left, I said "Thanks for your help, Mrs. Hanks."

"Shanks, not Hanks," she screeched with a shrill laugh.

She wasn't such a bad old doll, at that, I thought as we walked away. And at about the same time I found that I could smile again.

CHAPTER 9

Ever since boyhood, flying had held for me a hypnotic fascination. It was one of the supreme disappointments of my life that I failed to win my wings at Kelly Field and yet even this youthful tragedy hadn't cooled my enthusiasm. For I had gone on to get my ticket and, while I was to find my ability as a pilot of great use on occasion, I flew whenever I could primarily for my own enjoyment.

During the summer of 1930, and after Al Capone's return to Chicago, the pressures on us mounted constantly and the buildup of nervous tension at times became almost unbearable. I decided the only place I could get completely away from it all was to take to the air whenever I could find enough free time.

It felt almost like going home after a long absence as I drove into the Chicago airport and then began to wander among the hangars until I came to one at which a sign advertised:

"Acme Flying Service—Lessons and Rentals."

A freckled, blue-eyed man who wore stained coveralls and a permanent grin was tinkering with an open cockpit biplane and I asked him where I could find the boss.

"Right here," he told me. "Boss, owner, mechanic, instructor and anything else you want in this outfit. The handle's Tim Carroll. You want to take lessons or are you trying to collect a bill?"

We both chuckled and I told him I simply might be interested in renting his airplane from time to time.

"Don't dare go 'way until I get this cowling back on," he directed laughingly. "I don't get enough customers to

116

be able to afford to lose 'em but I gotta have this baby ready for a lesson this afternoon."

It wound up with me giving him a hand and afterwards we went over to the Greasy Spoon, a little restaurant used by airport personnel, and quickly became friendly over a cup of coffee. The upshot was that soon I had arranged to rent Tim's plane at my convenience. In the course of our conversation, I gave Carroll a rundown on my flying experience and told him that I was a prohibition agent.

"Hmph!" he snorted. "And some people are afraid of airplanes. Man, I'd rather fly around the world twice than tackle those Capone mugs."

His forehead puckered in deep thought as he tried to recall something and suddenly he snapped his fingers.

"Say, there's another one of your guys hangs out around here. Takes up a ship belonging to a friend of mine. Now let's see, what's his name?"

I was quite surprised at this information for I didn't know of any other prohibition agents in the regular Chicago bureau, and particularly on our squad, who flew.

"Seems to me the guy's name is Baylor," Tim said. "Baylor? No. Taylor? Yeah, that's it, Taylor."

"You mean Jim Taylor? A thin, quiet sort of fellow."

"That's the gent," Tim nodded.

Subsequently I took Mavis out to the airport for her first ride in an airplane and, as Tim checked over the plane, he told me that Taylor was somewhere around the airport right then. I hadn't seen him since learning from the freckle-faced Carroll that Taylor had the flying bug, too, so Mavis and I wandered over to the restaurant and there, indeed, sat the lean Jim.

"This is unexpected," I told him. "I didn't know you had a ticket."

"Just never had much time to talk to you about it," he replied with an amused look on his hollow-cheeked face. "I guess there's a lot of things get lost in the rush."

We talked for a while and then Taylor said he had to check back in at the office. He left and I went back to Acme, where Carroll had the plane all ready, and took the glowing-cheeked and slightly apprehensive Mavis for a ride.

It was a peaceful interlude in a rather hectic period. Because by this time, all of our groundwork was beginning to pay terrific dividends. There always seemed to be new leads from such sources as Mrs. Hanks, Jack Martin and our various telephone taps and we pulled off a series of raids which put a tremendous dent in the Capone operations.

The pattern was almost without deviation: a tip, a stakeout to make certain that we were on solid ground and then our devastating arrival with the armored truck.

The cost to the mob was growing enormous for the combined sum of our captured trucks, wrecked breweries, confiscated whiskey and scuttled beer was reaching staggering proportions. It stood to reason that Capone, a man noted for his homicidal rages and callous contempt of the law, would attempt deadly reprisals. The first came one afternoon when I went to pick up Leeson.

Joe just a short time earlier had moved out of his hotel on finding a comfortable ground floor apartment in a quiet, residential neighborhood. One of the incongruities I found in this iron-fisted ex-sailor, in addition to his soft heart for those in trouble or need, was that he liked to cook.

"You name it and I'll cook it as good as any woman you ever saw," he told me defiantly on one occasion when I found him in the kitchen baking a cake. "And you tell anybody about me wearing this apron and I'll break your skinny little neck."

Now, as I drove up to the apartment house in which he lived I was jolted to see a crowd gathered near his windows. As I got closer, I was startled to note that all of the windows were broken, the sashes hanging out grotesquely with bits of curtain dangling from their ragged edges.

"Federal man," I identified myself shortly to a policeman herding back the crowd of goggling onlookers. "What happened?"

"Somebody tossed a pineapple in the joint there," the policeman said.

"Oh, God," I groaned. "Anybody hurt?"

"I couldn't tell you, Mac. Maybe inside . . ."

I didn't hear the rest of it for I was running to the front entrance, the fear beating up in my throat that Joe might be lying there inside.

"Hey, Paul, over here."

I stopped short and breathed a deep sigh of relief at the familiar sound of Joe's voice. Then I saw him, talking to a lieutenant of police at one side of the lobby.

"You all right?" I asked him, grabbing one big arm.

"Yeah, but you should see what a mess it made out of the apartment. Blew it all to hell."

It had, indeed. The furniture was good now only for kindling. The only thing, oddly enough, which seemed undisturbed was a hand-worked sampler on the wall which proclaimed "God Bless Our Happy Home."

"Probably ruined the stove, too," Joe said sorrowfully, lowering his voice and gazing around surreptitiously before adding in an aside, "and I had the best damned pot of chili you ever tasted simmering on it."

I asked him how he had managed to escape the explosion.

"Hell, I wasn't even in there," he told me. "I'd gone down to the store to get some tabasco. The chili needed just a spot more. I heard this thing go boom clear around the block and I came back to see what it was all about and what do I see except that I've had visitors.

"Now," he added disgustedly, "it's back to that damned hotel where they won't even let you use a hot plate."

We had been lucky again but, I wondered, how long would our good fortune hold out.

"They're going to pay for this," Joe grunted vengefully as we gathered his few belongings and took them out to the car.

They did, too, and within the week.

The mob couldn't move beer without trucks, which are rather difficult to camouflage, and several nights later as we patrolled vigilantly Joe spotted a heavily loaded van which, from the looks of it, was toting only empty barrels.

"Don't get too close," Joe said. "I've got a hunch this dude is on his way to a brewery."

I laid well back and the truck wheeled around a corner toward a vehicular bridge over the railroad tracks. It was gone from view when we made the same turn. Nor was it in sight on the bridge, but then I spotted a side street which came to a dead end.

"It had to go down that street," I insisted. "But damned if I see it."

I turned into the street and drove slowly to the end of it. And there, sitting back from the street, was a large garage. Next door was a grimy looking all-night restaurant and I suggested we take a look inside.

A short order cook in a dirty apron was leaning on the counter with his elbows, reading a newspaper. We ordered coffee and I asked him:

"Got any idea what they do in that garage next door?"

"Not me," he said quickly. "I don't think they do anything there. Nope, as a matter of fact, it's empty."

When we went out, Joe said quietly: "He had a helluva time making up his mind, didn't he?"

We prowled the outside of the garage but it was dark and there wasn't a sound from inside. As we got around to the front again, the short order cook was standing curiously in the front door of the restaurant.

"Ah, the hell with it," Joe said loud enough for his benefit. "There isn't anything around here. Let's go."

"Looks like a dud to me," I corroborated as we got into the car.

But the next night, from the nearby incline which led down to the railroad tracks, we watched from the concealment of some tall weeds as several trucks entered light and departed with heavy loads.

We hit it at three-thirty the following morning, covering front, rear and roof. But when we crashed inside, there were two trucks which were almost loaded and the open ation obviously was in full swing. But there wasn't a soul in the place.

Going outside, I called up to Seager and Chapman on the roof.

"Hey, anybody come out that way?"

"Not a soul," Chapman yelled back.

We were completely puzzled and, while the inventory started, I walked outside with Leeson. We were just in time to see six men come out of the restaurant and start up toward the main road. They were all picking their teeth—too ostentatiously.

"Let's get 'em," I told Joe.

Ordering them back to the garage, we held them in a group on the sidewalk in front of the busted doors.

"What's a matter, you guys nuts?" one of them argued.

Just then, Mike King, who had been poking around the garage, called to us that he had found something.

"Get a load of this," he said when Joe and I went inside.

All I could see was a bunch of coats hanging on the wall. King swept them aside with the flourish of a magician pulling a rabbit out of a hat and there was a crude hole chopped into the wall which led right into the back room of the little restaurant next door.

"A switch on the Zibak garage," I told Mike. "Except this is a lot smaller and less complicated."

"Let's get the cook in the restaurant," Leeson suggested. "That's why we didn't see anybody in there the first night. He's got to be the lookout."

We were too late. The cook was long gone, leaving the restaurant wide open with the lights blazing.

Back in front of the garage, the six men we had collared were protesting vehemently that we couldn't hold them.

"Wait a second," said King, "I think I know how maybe we can pin it on these babies if they really were working here."

Taking Leeson and me aside, Mike explained quickly that he had been spending some spare time visiting with

Leonard E. Keeler at the Northwestern crime laboratory. Keeler was the inventor of the polygraph, the so-called lie detector, and a pioneer in the burgeoning art of scientific crime detection.

"Let's scrape some residue off of their shoes," King drawled in his soft, easy manner. "We'll get Keeler to analyze it because, if they have been working in there, they've got to have brewer's yeast ground into the soles of their shoes."

Walking out front, Leeson and I ordered the men to sit on the curb. Then, getting napkins from the restaurant, I took a penknife and scraped the men's shoes, marking each individual packet with the supposed violator's name.

They watched with extreme interest.

"What the hell you suppose he's doing?" one asked another.

"Damned if I know," was the reply. "I told you, I think these guys are nuts."

But King's revolutionary hunch paid off in spades. For, as it eventually developed, Keeler's analysis showed a heavy impregnation of brewer's yeast in the scrapings from each of the men's shoes and on this evidence they were found guilty.

While the others took the prisoners to the local precinct station and booked them, Chapman finished his inventory and left Leeson and me on guard until the arrival of the contract crew which would dismantle the place.

"Come on," Joe said, "that empty restaurant isn't doing anybody any good. I'll cook you some breakfast while we're waiting."

We went inside the restaurant and Joe whipped up a very tasty omelet.

"You'd better not ever get thrown into jail down in Greenville," I told him. "You cook too good."

"Why's that?" he asked.

As we ate, I told him about the time I had arrested a Negro in a raid on a still and, having a load of liquor to dispose of, I took the man to the county jail and told them I would come back later to file charges. I had to laugh when I thought about it, although it probably wasn't very funny to the man, because in some way I completely forgot about him.

I wasn't kidding when I told him that it was six months later before I remembered the arrest and, in some confusion went back to the county jail.

"What happened to that fellow I brought in six months ago?" I asked the sheriff.

"Oh," he said casually, "we still got him."

"My God, sheriff," I told him, "let him go."

The sheriff was adamant.

"Nothing doing," he said. "That boy's the best cook we've had in this jail in years and we're gonna keep him a while longer."

Joe choked over a mouthful of omelet.

"You know," I said honestly, "I had a helluva time getting them to set him free."

We had barely finished eating when Barney Doyle and his wrecking crew arrived on the scene. It was, for them, an unusually speedy appearance because they usually took their own sweet time showing up.

"How come you got here so quick?" I asked him.

"Hell," Barney said, "I only live a few blocks from ere." Then, setting his crew into motion, he added, "Well, I see you finally got this place."

In answer to our questions, Barney admitted that he had known all along that this particular brewery was in operation.

"It's been here more than three years," he said.

"Why in hell didn't you tell us?" Joe said.

Barney looked indignant.

"Why in hell should I tell you? You do your job and 'll do mine. I ain't paid to find these dumps for you."

He walked away grumbling. Joe just shook his head.

It was going on six o'clock in the morning by now and e were weary and, I thought, looked like bums. Long go we had turned to wearing old clothing when making ur raids. We both needed a shave and I presumed that e circles under my eyes were as dark as those under

Joe's. I tossed the tommygun I always carried during a raid on the back seat and we took off rapidly for home.

All of a sudden I realized we were going the wrong way on a one-way street and then, to compound my indiscretion, I slowed at a traffic light, saw nothing coming either way, and went on through its red glare.

A police whistle cut through the gray morning light behind us and I stopped and backed up. As the policeman walked up to the car I asked:

"What's it all about, officer?"

"Whatta yez mean, what's it all about?" he mocked me.

Then he looked into the car and spotted the tommygun on the back seat and it seemed that he jumped about three feet in the air. Clawing at his pistol, he finally got it out and pointed it at us, shouting:

"Be sure and come out of there with yer hands up, yez dirty buggers."

Don't ask me why, because there's nothing humorous about having a gun pointed at you. But Joe and I were suddenly almost hysterical with laughter. The more we laughed, the more the policeman waggled his gun and demanded that we get out of the car.

"Federal officers," Joe finally gasped, flipping his lapel to show his badge. "We're federal officers."

I thought the policeman was going to have a stroke.

"Federal officers are yez?" he roared, peering at the badge. "Yez are, God damned yez, and here's a ticket for going the wrong way and for crashing a light."

We gave it to Froelich the next day, with our compliments.

"Hell's bells," I laughed, "there's got to be some compensation for this kind of work and these kind of hours."

Froelich laughed too, as he took it.

But he wasn't laughing much in the next couple of months. For once again we began to come up with one dry hole after another. We were, we all knew, making good finds and yet, when we hit spots which noticeably had been in full swing, we found little or nothing. It began to gnaw at all of us.

"Damn it," Froelich said finally when he called us in for a general meeting, "I just can't understand it."

It was a tip-off on how worried he was because it was the first time I ever could recall having heard him swear.

There was a tight, tense atmosphere in the office after his outburst. None of us had to be told the implication behind his words because, I knew, it must be the top thought in everyone else's mind.

Was it possible we had another informer in our midst; that the mob, failing to frighten us off and finding us full of rabbit-foot luck, had gotten to one of our number once again?

"I can't believe it," I told Lesson later. "I'd bet my life on every one of these guys. As a matter of fact, we usually do whenever we go on a job."

Leeson gave me that familiar grunt, larded this time with an overtone of disdain.

"Don't kid yourself, junior. Somebody's selling out as sure as blazes."

If it was true, he was doing it smart. The taps showed nothing and, while I went so far as to take a chance on meeting Jack Martin in Mavis' apartment to personally shake him up, he could find out absolutely nothing.

It almost cost me my life and, by sheer chance, Mavis her life, too.

We had gone out to the airport for an afternoon flight, Mavis having become quite a flying enthusiast, and we had to wait because the freckled Tim Carroll told us he hadn't had time to check over the ship. While we were waiting, I suggested a bite of lunch and we went to the Greasy Spoon. Sitting at the counter was Jim Taylor, the quiet man of our squad who also was a nut on flying.

"Sit with us," I invited, but he told us he was just leaving and walked on outside.

Jim always had appeared non-communicative and a "loner." So I forgot about him and we ordered lunch.

Afterwards we walked back to Acme and a hanger-on whom I knew only as "Shorty" told me that Tim Carroll said to tell me that the plane was checked out and we could take it up. Tim was nowhere in sight and, not wanting to waste any more time, we taxied out and soon were airborne.

We usually flew for about an hour, heading out over the lake or off over the surrounding farm country, whichever our fancy dictated. This day we headed due west and Chicago had dropped from view behind us when suddenly the motor coughed once and died.

Dead stick landings are chancy at best but the luck in which we had been running held again. For below me, with the ground coming up fast, was a smooth, flat meadow and I sat her down with only a few minor bounces. Imagine, I thought, if we had been over the lake or this had been a field full of stumps or ravines.

Rapidly regaining her color, Mavis slipped off her shoes and walked barefooted as we hiked to a nearby farmhouse. From there I called Tim Carroll at Acme and told him about our emergency landing.

"Why'n hell did you take 'er up before I checked 'er out?" he complained heatedly.

"But," I protested, "that fellow, Shorty, told me you said it was okay."

Tim was unconvinced.

"I didn't say no such damned thing. I was fixin' to check it out right after you left for the Greasy Spoon. Then I get a phone call to appear at the administration office. Nobody there knows what it's all about and I waste a lot of time. Well, when I get back, you're gone."

Both of us were mystified but he told me to sit tight until he arrived and, after getting the directions for him, I hung up still puzzling over the jumbled chain of events.

The farmer invited us to have dinner while we waited for Tim and, when he arrived in a car driven by a friend, we went to the plane and he checked it over. His face was grim as he looked up from an inspection of the motor.

"Somebody's been messin' with it," he growled. "See, here's the marks of a wrench. They loused up the fuel line. You're damned lucky you didn't crash her takin' off."

Tim finally pronounced the motor back in shape and, just before we flew the plane out of there, I told him: "Wait'll I get my hands on that Shorty. I'll break his damned neck."

We landed back in Chicago without further incident and, while Mavis rested in Tim's miniature office, he and I went looking for Shorty.

"He's usually hanging around the dispatcher's office," Tim said.

"C'mon and we'll see what this is all about."

Shorty wasn't hard to find and he showed no concern at our approach. He even evinced surprise that we were looking for him.

"How come you told Mr. Robsky I said my plane was all checked out and he could take it up?" Tim snarled, grabbing Shorty by the jacket and doubling up a fist.

"Whatcha talkin' about?" Shorty bleated.

"You know," Tim ranted. "You told him I said he could take up the plane and he damned near washed it out."

Shorty looked startled.

"Well, that's what the guy said that you said I should tell him."

I was beginning to get ideas now.

"What guy, Shorty?"

"Why that fellow Taylor. I saw Tim leave and then I thought Taylor was checkin' out the plane. Cuz when I came up, he said that Tim had okayed it and for me to tell you when you came back. He gave me a buck to be sure to give you the message."

It was terribly difficult to believe. After all, while Taylor and I had been virtual strangers, we had worked through some tough spots together. But it was plain that he had lured Tim away and doctored the fuel line. Now I itched to get my hands on him.

"You seen him lately?" I demanded of Shorty.

"Last time I saw him he was going into the Stinson hangar."

Telling Tim I'd meet him back at his office when I

picked up Mavis, I hurried to the Stinson hangar even though by now it was quite late. I was fortunate in finding three men playing cards in a back room.

"Any of you fellows seen a guy named Jim Taylor around here today?" I asked.

"Sure did," a round-faced man beamed happily. "He was right here in this office, paid me $15,000 spot cash for one of our new models, and took it right off for a vacation trip to Mexico."

He might have gone there or to Canada, I reasoned ruefully as I walked back to pick up Mavis, but if I ever caught up to him he'd wish he had gone to hell without stopping.

Proof that Taylor actually had tried to kill me had cropped up that very day while we were at the airport. The long-non-productive wire taps suddenly started paying dividends again. For when I related my tale to Froelich the next day, he tossed a typewritten report to me.

"What you say explains this," he said.

It was a report by Friel on a phone call to Ralph Capone at the Montmartre. It could have been the prelude to my own obituary. It read:

"Lemme speak to Ralph."

"This is Ralph."

"I got good news for Snorky."

"Yes?"

"The guy who's been tippin' us agreed to one last big job."

"Yes?"

"It cost us another ten grand but he guaranteed to send one of 'em out in a blaze of glory."

"When?"

"Read the morning papers."

"Fine, I'll tell the boss."

It was quite clear to me that I had been the one slated for the "blaze of glory." Fate, or the luck we were riding so hard, simply had nullified the guarantee. And, in the process, we had rid ourselves of another defector.

Undeniable verification that Taylor had taken his payoff and ran was that overnight our raids began once again to strike pay dirt. And, as far as the mob was concerned, it was three strikes and out because as later developments proved we now were down to the hard core who really deserved the title "The Untouchables."

CHAPTER 10

We were really bearing down now in a relentless effort to dry up the mob's beer and liquor supply, a ceaseless campaign which had become almost an obsession with every man on our squad.

There was no question but that we were closing breweries faster than the syndicate could open them, smashing stills more quickly than they could be built and confiscating imported liquor at a speedier rate than they could run it in across the border from Canada.

There was a warm glow of satisfaction in Froelich's voice when he called a special meeting merely to congratulate us on the work the squad was accomplishing.

"I know you are driving yourselves," he sympathized, "and I hate to take the time out of your day. But I did feel that all of you should hear this wire tape recording which Friel made on a call to Jake Guzik at the Wabash Hotel."

Froelich beamed at us and then began to read.

"Jake?"

"Yes."

"Listen, that police captain with the mole on his cheek is in for his monthly payoff."

"Tell him he has to take a pass this month."

"He ain't gonna like it."

"I don't give a damn whether he does or not. We just haven't got it this month. The boss says everybody, and that means everybody, takes a pass this time around. Anyhow, what kind of protection does that bastard think

130

he's furnishin' us? Those damned feds are just about run-
nin' us out of business."

Froelich flipped the pad down on his desk with a broad
smile.

"Gentlemen, that's all there is to it. But it is a magnificent tribute to the work you have been doing, even if it
wasn't intended as one."

The aftermath of our very next raid was to prove how
desperate, indeed, the mob was becoming.

That same week, Joe and I were riding down South
Halstead Street when we drew up on a large, closed moving van which appeared perfectly legitimate. As we arrived at the intersection, the truck just made the traffic
light and we had to stop while the van continued on.

By the time the light changed we were almost a block
behind and, as we started to overhaul it, the truck swung
around a corner. I drove straight on past the intersection
but the sharp-eyed Leeson sat erect suddenly and directed
me to pull over to the side and park.

"What's up?" I asked in some surprise.

"I'm just curious," he said as he walked back toward
the corner. "That moving van turned here but, as we
passed the intersection, I looked up the block and it had
disappeared completely."

It was a commercial area of stores and office buildings
and, on the corner around which the truck had turned
there was a white eight-story building. Dominating the
ground floor was a bank but, as we walked down the side
street, we noticed that at the end of the building there was
a large metal door of the overhead type.

"Let's take a look around the back," Joe suggested,
leading the way up a driveway behind the building.

It was a dead-end loading zone and yet the van still
was nowhere in sight. Joe leaned back and craned his
head up at the outside of the building.

"Over there's a rear entrance of some sort into the
building," I pointed, and we strolled inside.

We found ourselves in a small, rear lobby which contained one elevator and, across from it, a tiny candy

stand. From behind a slender stock of wares, a grizzled little old man peered speculatively at us through his bifocals.

"We just want to use the elevator, Pop," I told him.

"Help yourself," he said in a cracked voice. "It's one of them new-fangled kind. Just press the button. Say, where you fellers goin'?"

"Upstairs," Joe grinned.

When the elevator descended in answer to our ring, we entered it and punched the buttons for every floor. As it creaked to a stop at the first floor, and the door opened, we saw with a quick look that these were all offices. It was the same way on the second and third floors, so we closed the door and started up again. But, when the door reopened, we were on the fifth floor.

"Hey," I questioned, "what the hell happened to the fourth floor?"

"Let's go see."

The elevator kept right on going up and, on each floor all the way to the top, it was merely one bank of offices after another. At the eighth, we punched the button for the fourth floor again. But the elevator went right on past four again and we found ourselves back in the rear lobby.

"The old geezer is gone," Joe pointed out.

"There's the stairway," I observed. "Let's walk up to four and see why they have such lousy elevator service."

We plodded up the stairs and when we came to the fourth floor landing found that the door was locked. Joe, ever impatient, waited only a few seconds after my knocking received no attention and then put his big foot to the door right at the lock. Two wallops and it sprang open.

We were completely amazed at what we had discovered.

Here, taking up the entire floor of this modern office building, was one of the largest breweries we had unearthed during our entire operation in Chicago. Huge vats lined the walls and the van which had disappeared with such suspicious rapidity down on the street looked incongruous sitting right there in that high-ceilinged room.

The metal door downstairs which had been closed and seemingly led into the back of the bank was actually a truck elevator which led to this one floor.

Investigation disclosed that there wasn't a soul in the place. It wasn't until later that we understood why. A scrutiny of the candy counter in the rear lobby revealed that the old man's stock was so old and dusty as to have been merely a decoy. Underneath the counter we located a button which sounded an alarm on the fourth floor. He had merely been a lookout and, when we were in the elevator, he had given a signal to those in the brewery and they had escaped by a narrow stairway which led out to the main street on the other side of the bank.

The rear passenger elevator, we found, had been geared so that it wouldn't stop at the fourth floor.

The mob had spent a tremendous amount of money on this setup, thinking to block us from crashing in with our steel-buttressed truck. But, by the merest chance and Leeson's vigilance, we had stumbled onto it and the two of us had been able to capture it with an absolute minimum of effort.

Chapman, after he had answered our summons and completed an inventory, set the value of the plant at $125,000.

This was a shocking body blow to the underworld, but the mob didn't take such losses lightly or without thought as to how it could recoup such a sum.

Our wire tap on the Montmartre disclosed immediately that the mob figured we had been tipped off. This was revealed by a caller who didn't identify himself in his conversation with Ralph Capone. This apparently was unnecessary and he came right to the point.

"We're lookin' for the leak."

"You'd better find it or the boss will have your hide."

"Look, Ralph, the only thing we can figure is that the rental agent sold us out."

"You aren't getting paid to think. Find out for sure."

With that, Capone had slammed down the receiver.

"We'd better investigate and ascertain who the rental

agent might be and put him on his guard," Froelich worried. "I'd hate to have an innocent party suffer for something which we discovered on our own."

Leeson and I checked up immediately and telephoned Froelich to forget his worries about the rental agent.

"The bank handled the rental," I told him.

We didn't figure it, but the bank should have been worried.

Because a week later there was a daylight stickup at the bank by a carload of thugs who escaped without a trace.

They got away with exactly $125,000.

The newspapers never connected the two incidents. But we tapped a call to Guzik, the mob's treasurer, at the Wabash Hotel the night of the robbery and the conversation was extremely illuminating.

"Jake there?"

"No."

"Well, just tell him we got back the big investment."

That was all. But we realized that the mob, getting desperate for cash, had evened accounts with the bank which they figured had sold them out.

It was only a short time later that I had an experience with another van which, to me, had humorous overtones. On a Sunday afternoon I had picked up Mavis and was driving down one of the busiest streets in Chicago when I pulled up alongside a truck at a traffic light. The thought never occurred to me that it was an unusual time and day for a moving van to be in the downtown area but for some unknown reason as the driver looked casually over at me, our glances met and I spontaneously wise-cracked to him:

"Hey, buddy, I'm a federal agent. Is that thing loaded with beer?"

Mavis and I both stared open mouthed as the driver flung open the door of the truck, leaped out and raced away down the street as fast as he could go.

Right then and there, while the cars behind us began blowing their horns impatiently, I jumped out of my car and going around to the back of the abandoned van opened the door.

It was loaded to capacity with barrels of beer.

A burly Irish traffic cop appeared at my shoulder, an apoplectic look on his weather-beaten face.

"What the hell's going on here?"

"I'm a prohibition agent," I told him. "The driver of this thing just hauled his freight and left me here with a load."

The policeman, feet spread and fists bunched on his hips, glared at me and his voice dripped with sarcasm.

"Now ain't that just dandy?" Then, his voice turning to a roar, he added: "The hell with this prohibition stuff. Just get this thing t'hell outta here so I can get this traffic moving."

Mavis couldn't drive and the policeman turned the air blue with blistering language which was punctuated by the raucous blare of automobile horns as I hurriedly parked my car. Then I grabbed Mavis by the hand and, after helping her up into the cab of the truck, finished our Sunday ride by driving the van full of beer down to our office at the Transportation Building.

To top it off with a hilarious note, enroute we passed a couple of the pearl-gray hats—and they waved a friendly greeting.

"I always thought," Mavis smiled brightly, "that there was a certain raffish air about you. That certainly substantiates my theory."

I grinned and told her that I wasn't too certain about myself, but that the truck driver who had escaped must have felt kind of like a mountaineer I once had pursued on foot in South Carolina after surprising him at his still. He had taken off like a jack rabbit in a forest fire, with me right on his heels. We went up over a ridge and right down past his cabin and there stood his wife on the porch, wringing her hands tearfully.

"Run, Rafe, run!" she had screamed. "You ain't no good to me in jail you son of a bitch."

Mavis, who was thoroughly enjoying the whole experience, laughed delightedly and asked me if I had caught the mountaineer.

"Nope," I admitted. "He could run even faster than the fellow who was driving this truck."

Leeson, when I saw him the next day, kidded me about letting the truck driver get away.

"You think you could have handled it better?" I needled.

"I was just about to get around to that," he mouse-trapped me. "I'm about to take in a whole fleet of trucks at one fell swoop, junior, and if you promise not to let anybody escape why I'll take you along with me."

Joe, it developed, had come up with a tip on a public garage where the mob transferred liquor from a large truck to a number of small trucks and cars for delivery. We drove over there and pulled right inside and parked. There was only one attendant and, after a quick check disclosed a load of liquor in a big truck, we told him to just sit in the inner office and keep his mouth shut. Joe took out insurance by simply pulling the only phone completely off its wall bracket.

We were sitting in one of the trucks in a spot which commanded a view of the whole place when another man entered carrying a bulky box. It turned out to be a lettering kit.

"They told me it was about time to put a bunch of new names on the trucks," he told us as we approached him.

"Go right ahead," Joe agreed. "You know which trucks, don't you?"

"Oh, sure," the painter nodded.

We strolled back to our original vantage point and sat there watching him as he proceeded busily with his lettering, the fresh paint identifying every truck in the fleet for us. The workman was about finished when three men drove in and, while we sat there watchful and unobserved, one of them directed the two others in the transfer of cases of whiskey from the large truck to the smaller ones. The leader we recognized as a mobster named Bob Angelo, right-hand man to Joe Fusco, one of the big shots in the Capone mob.

Sitting at ease, we let them work up a little sweat before stepping out and collaring all three of them.

When Angelo ultimately came to trial, I had to appear on the witness stand against him. His lawyer was an attorney named John Powers, a slick-talking, dapper man who subsequently was disbarred for unethical practice in connection with mob activities. Powers had a reputation for being particularly nasty on cross-examination but when he appeared in the courtroom I knew that this was one gent for whom I was ready and waiting.

I made it a practice throughout my career of always carrying one of those vest-pocket type diaries in which I faithfully recorded conversations, wire-tap information, names, telephone numbers, details of raids and any other incidents or data which I considered significant or meaningful.

Noted carefully in this diary were the results of a wire tap I had worked briefly some time earlier on Joe Fusco's phone. Ultimately we had decided to discontinue it because it was nonproductive but when I saw Powers my mind shot back to that tap and I carefully plotted my own little pitfall for him.

For, when he began to cross-examine me, I innocently pulled forth my little diary and started referring to it as if I was confused concerning various points in my testimony.

"What's that?" he asked sharply, pointing at the diary.

"A notebook in which I keep notes on various cases," I explained artlessly. "We handle so many that I have to refer to it to refresh my memory. Is it all right?"

Powers was blandly agreeable, for he knew, as I did also despite my seeming naivete, that once I referred to the notebook under the laws of jurisprudence he would have the right to cross-examine me on the whole diary. Certainly, I had figured, he would assume that in this manner he might garner some valuable information.

"Now, Mr. Robsky," he orated with a sly showmanship intended to demonstrate to all observers the manner in which he had ensnared me, "will you read us some excerpts from your notebook please?"

"Any particular day?"

"No, just pick something at random," Powers directed with theatrical relish.

It took me but a moment to locate what I wanted without seeming to search for anything in particular.

"Well, here's one about a conversation I heard on a wire tap on the telephone of Joe Fusco," I recited, not needing to identify Fusco for any of those present.

"Read it," Powers ordered, although now there was a note of restraint barely evident in his tone.

I cleared my throat and raised my voice so that everyone would be certain to hear me clearly.

"This call came in for Fusco and the caller said 'This is Johnny' and Fusco said 'Johnny who?' and the caller said . . ."

Powers interrupted with smooth haste.

"That will be enough."

But the judge leaned over the bench and intoned:

"Continue to the end of that, Mr. Robsky."

"Your honor, I object," Powers roared.

"Objection overruled. Continue, Mr. Robsky."

Powers began pacing back and forth as I went on.

". . . and the caller said 'This is Johnny Powers, dammit. Don't you even know your own lawyer?' And . . ."

Again Powers leaped forward, his face crimson and consternation clearly apparent in voice and manner.

"That will be enough, Mr. Robsky."

Again the judge waved him to silence.

"Mr. Powers, this court has ordered the witness to read to the end of that passage. You will be so good as to refrain from interruption or I shall be forced to hold you in contempt of court."

"Objection," Powers stormed. "Wire-tap evidence is not admissible and . . ."

"Objection overruled," the judge glared. "You demanded this same information under cross-examination

and now the court intends to hear it. Continue, Mr. Robsky."

Again I took up where I had left off.

"Fusco was very apologetic and then asked the caller
what he wanted. This man who identified himself as
Johnny Powers said 'I need sugar and I need it damned
quick or some of your hoods are going to rot in jail.' "

I looked up into the furious scowl Powers had fixed on
me and grinned right in his face. Then, as I started to
speak again, he leaped forward and raised another objection.

"Objection sustained," the judge nodded, grinning at
me as he said it.

We both knew that I had made my point, and I guess
everybody else in the courtroom did, too. It was a highly
satisfying bit of byplay all the way around, as far as the
forces of law and order were concerned, and made quite a
hit with the jury, too, because we got a quick conviction.

When the trial came to a close, the judge summoned
me to his chambers. Confidentially, he told me that he really had enjoyed putting Powers on the spot.

"Powers is riding for a fall," he predicted, revealing
that the bar association for some time had been investi-
gating the attorney's gangland connections and machina-
tions. "But he won't forget the manner in which you held
him up to public ridicule and, with his connections, I'd be
very careful if I was you, Mr. Robsky."

"Thank you, your honor," I concurred. "I learned a
long time ago when I was breaking into this business
down in South Carolina that you can't ever hold anybody
lightly, not even the uneducated ones.

"We had a gnarled old mountaineer named Jed we
used on a number of jobs," I explained to the judge as he
leaned back and lit a cigar. "One day we were riding out
of town on some mission or other and we saw a huge billboard advertising the imminent arrival of the circus.

"The sign said 'Coming—Ringling Brothers Circus—
Greatest Show On Earth—Sept. 1.' "

Old Jed, who had taught himself to read in a painstaking, haphazard fashion, laboriously spelled out the words on the billboard, I related to the attentive jurist, and then he turned to me with a puzzled grimace.

"What do you s'pose is the greatest show on earth?"

"Why," I told him in some surprise, "I guess it's that one. Anyhow, it says so."

"No it don't," old Jed insisted stubbornly. "It says it's the greatest show on earth—'cept one."

One of the other men with us started to laugh at Jed, but I shut him up by telling the old mountaineer that maybe he was right after all.

"Later on," I recounted, "old Jed came up with a lot of information which he fed to me privately. One day when I asked him why he was so cooperative, he said 'Ah guess 'cause you was nice to me, Paul, the day that smart aleck done tried to make a fool out'n me.' "

The judge was amused at my tale but sobered quickly.

"Some people remember the nice things you do for them," he allowed philosophically, "but if I were you I'd remember that even more often people seem to harbor memories of what has been done against them. I guess it's just human nature."

He didn't have to impress this fact on me. And, if I had needed a lesson in caution as well as an indication of the hair-trigger, unforgiving temper of the mob, it was provided for me a few nights later when Joe and I were sitting in a basement restaurant on the South Side ostensibly having dinner but actually casing the place in an attempt to determine whether it was a speakeasy.

Both of us tensed, ready for almost anything, as the street door at the top of the flight of stairs leading down into the restaurant was flung open violently and two men were catapulted down the steps head over heels.

Their faces and clothing were covered with blood as they wound up in a sobbing heap on the bottom landing.

We were shocked. As incredible as it seemed, their ears had been cut off.

They were, as it developed, a couple of young neighborhood punks who had no connection with the mob. The restaurant owner summoned a doctor who lived a few doors away and, while he patched them up, one of the toughs groaned out his sad story.

"We was in a 'speak' last night and when we come out there was this truck loaded with beer sittin' there," he moaned. "Me and Frankie here is feelin' pretty high and we think it's a real gag to drive the truck away. We didn't hurt it or nothin'. Just parked it in an alley a couple blocks away and go back and watch the fun. We watch the driver have a fit for a while, laughin' like hell at 'im, and then finally we tell 'im what we did and where he can find his lousy truck."

Ashen-faced, he paused as if considering the cost of those laughs. Then he continued.

"That's all we did. But tonight four hoods picks us up like they're gonna take us for a ride but they take us in the alley and, God have mercy, they did this to us."

Leeson wasn't one to let an opportunity pass.

"You fellows want to get even?" he asked quietly as the doctor went to wash his hands. "Maybe you can tell us where they get their beer?"

The bigger one, who had been doing all the talking, was fearfully suspicious.

"Who are you guys?"

"We're a couple of feds," Joe said, palming his badge, "and we'll guarantee we won't let anybody know where we got the tip."

The little one called Frankie shivered and drew back from us as if we had a contagious disease. There was terror in his whining voice.

"We better keep quiet, Joey. Maybe we get worse than this."

"T'hell with 'em," snapped the one called Joey, fingering his bandages. "Those bastards are gonna pay for this." Then he turned back to us. "Okay. I don't know where they got their beer but I do know where there's a helluva lot of booze stashed away."

Quickly, as if he was afraid that he might change his

mind, he babbled out an address. Then they bolted up the stairs and out the door. We never saw them again.

But we did find the liquor drop and it was a big one which, as Joe commented like a bullfighting afficionado, "was well worth four ears."

At first, when we crashed inside, we thought that the earless punk had given us a bum tip for the building appeared to be empty. But as we walked back toward the rear we passed over a section of flooring made out of wood. The rest of the floor was concrete.

"Sounds hollow," I observed as we stamped on it.

Close inspection uncovered a hidden ring bolt and underneath of the wooden flooring was a stairway which led down into a subterranean chamber as large as a two-car garage. It was so filled with cases of imported whiskies that we were barely able to squeeze down inside.

As we emerged from the cellar, a police car pulled into the doorway to the building and a red-faced sergeant who had helped us out on several occasions by taking prisoners to the local precinct house walked toward us.

"Hi," he welcomed us. "Find anything in this dump?"

I bobbed my head. "Some damned good whiskey, imported and uncut."

"Well, now," he grinned, "seems like a shame to destroy all of it."

I smiled back at him.

"It does at that, doesn't it?"

We turned our backs while he and his sidekick put a couple of cases of scotch into the squad car. They waved their thanks and left.

And within fifteen minutes we were besieged by three more squad cars and four patrolmen in a paddy wagon.

"Okay if we help you with the evidence?" asked one of them significantly.

Leeson looked at me and shrugged.

"Hell, why not!"

We had to step in and call a halt finally or we wouldn't have had any evidence left, for they were loading the cars and the patrol wagon with unrestrained vigor.

"Thanks a lot," one of them said as he lugged out the last case we let them have. "You guys made a real nice find."

"It was nice before you guardians of the law got here," Leeson ribbed him. "But good luck to you, and have a merry Christmas."

Joe and I latched onto a few bottles, too, before the cache was destroyed. Then, as we drove away quite satisfied with ourselves, I told him it reminded me of a find I had made down in Greenville one time just before the holidays.

"Okay, okay," Joe chuckled. "What's the story this time?"

"Well," I recounted, "my old boss, Austin, was always trying to teach me how to read 'travel' as they call a trail left by someone in the mountains. I wasn't having much success and I guess he thought I was pretty dumb or, at least, not very observant."

On this one particular day, I told Joe, we were going down the side of a mountain with me trailing along behind Austin when I spotted a cluster of fat, juicy wild blackberries. They had been as big as the end of my thumb and I couldn't resist the urge to eat a few. They were so sweet and juicy that I pushed my way into the brambles to reach another patch of them.

"Hey, Mr. Robsky," Austin called. "Come on, let's get out of here."

"All right," I replied. "I'll be along in just a minute."

"Well hurry up," he shouted, seeming quite unexpectedly impatient and, somehow, even a trifle anxious.

Just as I was about to leave the briar patch and follow Austin on down the trail, I related to the listening Joe, I happened to see what appeared to be a path leading farther into the brambles. This sure looks like "travel," one of those hidden and therefore suspect trails, I had thought, and I pushed on into the center of the bramble patch which covered some four acres of ground.

"I was pretty proud of myself," I narrated. "For there, concealed in the center of this natural barbed wire barrier were fifty large barrels of fermenting blackberry mash. So I fired a couple of signal shots to bring Austin back and he finally appeared, cussing the briars. I was extremely surprised that he didn't seem overly enthusiastic about my discovery but I rubbed it into him that I had found some 'travel' he had missed.

"Old man Austin just grunted grumpily," I laughed in retrospect. "But I hadn't been so smart at that. My discovery had deprived Greenville and most of the surrounding territory of its blackberry brandy for the Christmas season. And old man Austin, who missed very little that went on in the mountains, was particularly fond of having his blackberry brandy during the holidays."

Joe shook his head in mock resignation.

"You and your mountain memoirs. You certainly are a very lucky man that nobody has had the foresight to cut off my ears."

It was a sobering thought.

CHAPTER II

The growing desperation within the mob as result of our intensive operations was brought home to us in a roundabout fashion through a series of events which transpired after Leeson showed up at my apartment early one afternoon with news of unexpected aid.

Leeson explained to me that he had received a telephone call from one of the agents assigned to the permanent Chicago Bureau.

"He said he thought he was on to something big," Joe related. "He wanted to get together with me and I told him to meet us here at your place. Fellow named Milton Bernstein."

Bernstein, Joe told me with firm certainty, was one of the relatively few agents assigned to the Chicago Bureau who undoubtedly was on the square. They had worked together in Detroit for a brief period and Joe vouched for Bernstein without hesitation.

I liked the appearance of the man when he finally did arrive. Bernstein was muscular and square-set with black, curly hair and a direct manner of looking at anyone to whom he was talking. Our glances met squarely and his handclasp was firm and strong. He didn't waste any time on unnecessary preliminaries.

"I believe I've got something pretty good," Bernstein explained, adding with a wry look, "something that I don't want to get 'lost' like it sometimes does in our office. Anyhow, I know I can count on Leeson if it does develop like I expect it to."

"Paul, too," Leeson interjected abruptly.

Bernstein nodded his acceptance of Joe's recommendation of me and went on in a deep voice which reflected, as he confirmed later, that he was a native of Brooklyn.

"For quite some time I've been getting information from a stoolie known as 'Georgie the Gimp.' Mostly it's ordinary run-of-the-mill stuff and he'll usually settle happily for a ten spot. But 'The Gimp' called me last night and wants me to meet him at ten o'clock tonight in the underpass near the South Street Station."

"I know the place," Leeson inserted. "But what makes you think his information might be so hot this time?"

Bernstein grinned knowingly.

"Money. 'The Gimp' says what he's got is worth a hundred bucks. And a hundred bucks to Georgie is nothing less than a small fortune. Also, I might add, it ain't exactly hay to me but I happen to know that the guys on your squad pretty much have the freedom to make any expenditures you feel necessary. To be honest, I need your hundred bucks almost as much as I need you."

Bernstein chuckled when he said it, and we did, too.

We all knew without saying that if Bernstein obtained that kind of money in the regular bureau, the word probably would have been all over town within the hour.

As Bernstein had conjectured, we had no difficulty getting the money from Froelich and I had the hundred dollars tucked away in my pocket when we met Milt that evening.

Driving to the meeting place designated by "Georgie the Gimp," we took the precaution of parking near a little corner delicatessen about two blocks from the underpass. When we arrived, Bernstein suggested that one of us wait in the car because if there were too many of us it might either frighten off "The Gimp" or possibly attract decidedly unwelcome attention. It was his party, so Joe volunteered to stay behind.

Acting as nonchalantly as possible, Bernstein and I then slowly strolled the several blocks and the sounds of our footsteps echoed hollowly as we walked down into the dimness of the underpass.

"Georgie the Gimp," a gaunt, short, gray-haired man who dragged one foot when he walked and had a furtive manner about him stepped out of a dark cul de sac as we approached the center of the underpass. He jabbed a nervous finger in my direction and his voice dripped suspicion.

"Who's this guy?"

"One of our men," Bernstein said and then, as "The Gimp" showed an obvious reluctance to my presence, added quickly, "Not from the regular office. He's one of the special squad. You know, the ones they call 'The Untouchables.'"

"Georgie the Gimp" relaxed visibly.

"Oh," he breathed, "that's okay then. Everybody knows they're on the level."

What would he say, the thought flashed through my mind, if he had known about the ones who hadn't been 'untouchable.' But then "The Gimp's" voice brought me back to the moment.

"Where's the dough?"

"Just a minute," Bernstein protested. "Prove to us that what you've got is worth a hundred bucks."

"The Gimp" took a quick look around the deserted underpass and lowered his voice to a cautious whisper.

"I got big news. It's worth a hundred easy."

Bernstein shrugged impatiently.

"All right. If it's worth a hundred, you'll get it. Now spit it out."

"The Gimp" looked about surreptitiously.

"Well, I can tell you where they're landing most of the booze they bring in by boat from Canada. And somethin' else."

"All right," I urged. "Let's have it."

"There's a spot on the lake a few miles above Evanston," he said hoarsely. "Bascombe's Landing. That's where they land most of the stuff that comes by boat. But that ain't all. The way I get it, they're supposed to be holdin' a big pow-wow sometime soon, big shots from all over, and one of 'em is supposed to have been up in

Canada for somethin' and is comin' in along with one of the loads."

"Who's the guy?" Bernstein demanded sharply. "When's he get here?"

"Damned if I know," the Gimp swore. "That's all I know. But ain't it worth a hundred, now ain't it?"

I felt sorry for this fearful little man but, it struck me, we could kill two pigeons with one brick if we could ascertain just when the mysterious big shot was arriving.

"I'll tell you what," I asserted in a voice which told him I'd brook no argument. "You've got only half of what we want. So we'll give you fifty dollars and if you can find out when this big shot is coming in, we'll give you the other fifty."

"The Gimp" grimaced disgustedly but shoved forth a grimy paw and I counted fifty dollars into it.

"I'll call you," he whispered hoarsely, and scuttled rapidly away.

Bernstein and I walked out of the underpass and, climbing into the car, told Leeson what we had learned.

"You think he'll come through with what we want?" Joe asked Bernstein.

"For fifty bucks that guy would steam open Capone's mail in Hell's kitchen," Bernstein grunted.

Leeson grinned and, with some amusement, told us that he hadn't exactly been idle while we were gone.

"Some young punk comes up to the car and says 'You're a dick, ain't you?' I told him to go chase himself but he hung around a while, asking me what I was doing down here. Just a nosey young bastard. Wore the fanciest wrist support you ever saw. You know, one of those leather bands the kids think make 'em look like he-men. But this one had imitation rubies all over it."

We dismissed Joe's young punk from our minds and for the next several days, while Bernstein returned to his regular duties, Joe and I went on a fruitless prowl for action. Then, on a Wednesday afternoon, Bernstein called us to meet him that evening.

"Georgie says he's got what we want," Bernstein told

us as we drove once more to the underpass. "But he wouldn't give it to me on the phone. With him, it's cash on the barrelhead."

Parking where we had on our earlier visit, and once again leaving Joe in the car, Milt and I retraced our former route to the underpass and as before found "The Gimp" awaiting us in the silent shadows. He wasn't wasting any time, being intent on collecting his money and getting out of there as rapidly as possible.

"Tomorrow night they come in," he said. "I don't know who it is, but it's midnight tomorrow night at Bascombe's Landing. Now, gimme the fifty bucks."

I handed it over without a word and, dragging his lame leg, "Georgie the Gimp" made surprising time as he vanished in the opposite direction.

Returning to the car, we apprised Leeson of the information we had obtained and arranged for the three of us to meet the next night. As we drove Bernstein to where he wanted to go, Leeson revealed that while he was waiting for us he had another visit from the same young punk who wore the fancy wrist guard.

"Do you think he might have been an eye for the mob?" I wondered.

"No," Joe shrugged. "Just a dumb punk with a big curiosity bump."

Again we dismissed thoughts of Joe's visitor and, primarily intent on the next night, decided after some discussion that the three of us should be able to handle this job without calling in the remainder of the squad.

"Hell, there's only one big shot," Joe grunted in conclusion. "Maybe a few hoods and some booze, but it all will be right out in the open."

We met as planned at nine o'clock the next night and began our drive to Bascombe's Landing through a light rain which gradually turned into a steady downpour. Advance inquiries which we had made disclosed that we were to turn off on a deserted dirt road about five miles north of Evanston.

"There's a big sign on the corner," my informant had

advised. "You can't miss it. It's a damned lonely spot, though, that Bascombe's Landing."

He was right about it being lonely in that area, but not about it being easy to locate. For either a storm had blown down the sign he mentioned or else somebody had taken the precaution of removing it. Because we missed the turnoff and spent several hours driving aimlessly around in the rain and darkness trying to locate the intersection we were seeking.

It was just past midnight and I was beginning to think we might miss the boat, literally and figuratively, when we happened on a narrow, bush-bordered road whose ruts were filled with rainwater. Joe jumped out of the car and played the beam of his flashlight into the darkness beside the road.

"Okay," he said with gusty satisfaction as he jumped back into the car, "this is it. The damned sign is laying over there in the bushes."

I turned in and we jounced slowly along the road, speed being impossible on it anyhow, as we wound back in among the trees toward the lake shore. We were forced to go even more slowly when I cut the lights so that those at the landing wouldn't be warned of our approach.

I was startled when Milt, sitting beside me and peering out tensely with his nose pressed to the windshield, let out a sudden yell.

"Look out! There's another car!"

Creeping toward us, also without lights, was another car. Both of us halted barely in time, our radiators only a few feet apart. Instantly I snapped on my lights and saw two white blobs behind the windshield of a curtained touring car.

I had barely stopped when we were piling out of our car. Bernstein raced up to the driver's side while I sloshed up to the other side, ripping off the front curtain with one sweeping motion. Leeson, who had been riding in the back seat behind me, played it smart. He stayed by the front fender of our car so that he could see the other one in the glare of our headlights without himself being blinded or outlined.

Bernstein, too, had torn off the side curtain on the driver's side and we covered the four men inside with our pistols. Behind us, Joe commanded the whole situation with a ready tommygun.

Inside the car, I saw with a raking glance, were four of the pearl-gray hats.

The driver was a blue-jowled hoodlum with a built-in sneer. Sitting beside him, my pistol only inches from his head, was a heavy-set, well-dressed man whose eyes were round behind thick glasses. Instantaneously he had raised both empty hands against his chest, fingers extended and palms forward, to demonstrate clearly that he was unarmed.

The two in the back seat obviously were thugs. And if I required any further proof, the tommyguns clutched across their laps were all the evidence I needed.

"We're federal agents," I addressed the heavy-set man with the thick glasses. I had been trying to place him, for he was vaguely familiar, and then I recognized him as Meyer Lowenstein, one of the syndicate bosses from New York.

"Glad to see you made it on time for the meeting," I told him with a grin.

"Gentlemen," he said unctuously. "What can we do for you? As you can see, we're only a party of traveling businessmen."

"Yeah, and what a business," I cracked.

Then from the back seat came a quick flood of Yiddish, interrupted with sudden harshness by Bernstein from where he was standing vigilantly on the other side of the car.

"You try it," Milt snapped, "and it'll be the last move you'll ever make."

The heavy-set one in the front seat, keeping his hands elevated rigidly against his chest, swiveled his head and barked at the triggermen in the back seat.

"Shut up! That guy understands Yiddish."

"Damned right I do," Bernstein rapped out. "That monkey in the back," he raised his voice so that I could hear him clearly, and so that Leeson could, too, "wants to know whether they should blast us."

"All right, out of the car," I ordered Lowenstein.

It was a mistake. Almost a fatal one.

Lowenstein and the driver opened their doors simultaneously, as did the two gunmen in the back seat. Then, when the syndicate boss and the driver emerged, their bodies and the opened rear doors with their side curtains still on, completely screened the two getting out of the tonneau of the car.

The one on my side hurled himself into the bushes beside the rutted road and I dropped instinctively into the mud as he cut loose with a burst from his tommygun.

It was a fatal mistake for him.

Because Leeson, standing by the front fender of our car, loosed one long burst in the flood of the headlights and when he stopped spraying the bushes there was no sound except that of the falling rain and the fading echo from the deadly chatter of his tommygun.

The tense tableau came alive as I rose up off my muddy knees while Leeson splashed his way into the bushes. Within moments he reappeared.

"He's dead," Joe grunted flatly.

We disarmed the three others and herded them into the glare of our headlights. Then, after Bernstein backed the mobsters' car off the narrow road, we ordered them to walk back the way they had come while we followed them in our car.

"One move out of any of you bastards and you'll get the same thing that other bum got," Leeson warned.

Slowly they trudged through the rain, with us right on their heels, and within ten minutes we came out into a large clearing on the banks of the lake. Dimly we perceived the ghostly outline of three large trucks which investigation disclosed were partially loaded. And several hundred cases of whiskey were stacked high on a dock jutting out into the murky water.

But there was no one in sight: no boat, no loaders, no truck drivers. The noise of our fusillade had frightened them away and I could picture them fleeing back up the lake through the rain-shrouded night aboard their boat.

By now Lowenstein had found his oily voice again.

"You don't have a thing on us," he tried. "You didn't get us with this load and we were only defending ourselves back there when you started shooting."

I was muddy, wet and cold and my temper was close to the surface.

"Shut up," I told him angrily. "We'll find plenty of charges to stick on you, don't worry about that. Now clam up before I forget I'm not supposed to belt a guy who wears glasses."

He shut up.

We held a hurried conference and Bernstein volunteered to stay behind and guard the whiskey while Leeson and I drove our three prisoners to the lockup and arranged for the liquor to be taken away.

As we rode back out the narrow road, with the three prisoners sitting silently in the rear under the threat of Joe's ready pistol, we again passed the spot where the dead gangster lay in the bushes.

It brought back to my mind a time in South Carolina when we had raided a still and, in the melee, one of the moonshiners had been shot to death. Austin had gone to a small settlement nearby and attempted to hire an old mountaineer to take the body down the mountain in his mule-drawn wagon.

"How much you gonna charge?" Austin asked.

"Five dollars," the mountaineer replied.

Austin was indignant.

"Ain't that a mite high?" he demanded.

"Well, maybe t'is, at that," the mountaineer had reflected. "Ah'll tell yo' what. Let me tote down a load of likker at the same time and ah'll make it cheaper."

Muddy suit and all, I chuckled at the memory.

"What's so funny?" Leeson asked.

"Oh, nothing," I grinned. "Just thinking, that's all. Maybe I'll tell you about it some time."

There was nothing humorous, however, about the aftermath of this night's foray. And it was a development which proved that the mob also had us under constant, secret surveillance.

Because several days later when I picked up Leeson, Joe had a newspaper in his hand and, frowning, he said: "I want to take a run down to the morgue."

"Anybody I know?"

"Nope. But I think it's somebody I know. Listen to this."

Joe opened the newspaper and began to read.

"Gangland guns claimed another victim last night, the third this month, when the body of an unidentified man was found in the underpass near the South Street Station. The man had been shot three times through the head. The only lead to his identity was a jeweled wrist guard he was wearing."

"You think . . .?" I queried.

"Yep," Joe nodded. "I think it might be the young punk who talked to me both nights when I was waiting for you and Milt. It's possible that the mob was watching us somehow and thought he was the one who tipped us off. Anyway, I'd just like to make sure."

We rode in silence to the morgue and there, after identifying ourselves, were led into the cold storage room.

"Know him?" asked the attendant after he threw back the sheet which covered the body.

"No," Joe shook his head. "I can't help you."

But, once outside Joe drew a deep breath and helpless anger rode his voice.

"I didn't know his name but that was him. Another case where curiosity killed the cat. Just a nosey punk and he gets it by accidental design. But that's the way those bastards are. No mercy. I know."

I knew, too, that he was thinking about his own kid brother and I pitied the hood who happened to get in his way while Joe was in this black mood.

There was no question in our minds, however, but that the luckless punk had been the victim of a case of fatally mistaken identity.

It was shortly afterwards, curiously enough, that we had a double-barreled case of mistaken identity, too, but on this occasion it had the overtones of a Keystone Kop comedy.

Froelich had called us in and asked Leeson and me to go to a small town just across the Indiana line to check out some information on Al Capone. We arrived late in the afternoon and had no difficulty locating the local police station. The chief of police, a portly oldster who wore spectacles, was just about to leave when we entered.

"We're federal agents," I told him. "We'd like to get some information."

As I said it, I handed him my Justice Department identity card and, holding it in his hand, he led the way into his tiny office.

"Have a chair," he waved in friendly fashion and plumped himself into a creaking swivel chair behind a battered desk.

Pulling a chair close to the desk, I tossed a Chicago Police Department mug shot of Capone on top of a litter of papers and then sitting down started to question the old chief.

"You ever seen that guy?" I began.

He squinted with puzzled concentration at the picture he held in his hand.

"Now, you know, I seen this here feller some place or another," he pondered, "but I just can't seem to place him. One thing sure, though, he's a mean lookin' bastard, ain't he?"

I was startled as Joe began to roar with laughter.

"You . . ." Leeson spluttered. "It's you. He's lookin' at your identification card."

The chief turned red as fire and I had to swallow a grin over his discomfiture.

"Well, now . . ." he began.

"That's all right," I told him. "Leeson here sometimes calls me worse than that. The picture I mean is this one."

Hastily I reclaimed my I.D. card and, picking up the ignored mug shot of Capone handed it over to the chief. He gave it a quick look and nodded brisk recognition. His voice was positive.

"Al Brown. Yes, sir, that's who this is. He was pimping for a whorehouse here. Bouncer for it, too, 'til we ran all them fellers out of town."

We knew that "Al Brown" was one of the aliases Al Capone had used during his early days in the Chicago area. But the next thing the old police chief said stopped us cold.

"Yep, ran him out we did. Y'know, I often wondered whatever became of him."

I recovered my voice first and a quick look showed me Leeson's mouth hanging open in astonishment.

"Don't you ever read the papers?" I asked the chief. "That's Al Capone, the big shot in Chicago."

The chief was completely nonplussed. He made only one comment.

"Well I'll be damned."

Leeson seconded the motion.

Our trip was, from an information standpoint, a complete failure. The chief was unable to check out our information and we left.

"Can you imagine him not knowing Capone?" Leeson mused wonderingly as we drove back toward Chicago. "I wonder what Scarface Al would say about that? You know, maybe we ought to tell him."

I shot a quick side glance at Leeson. When he got that kind of a notion in his mind I knew he was just the kind who might think it would be a good idea to carry out.

Which, still brooding about the innocent punk who had been taken for a one-way ride, was exactly what my hard-rock partner was seriously contemplating.

CHAPTER 12

I had long since learned that when Joe Leeson got an idea in that craggy, leonine head of his there was nothing left to do but sit back and wait for the fireworks. So I wasn't too surprised when, a few days after our visit to the Indiana police chief, Joe suggested one afternoon that we drop in and look around the Lexington Hotel.

The first thought which flashed through my mind was that now I'd know exactly how Daniel felt when he stepped into the lion's den. Because the Lexington was the heart of the Capone empire, the throne room of the scarfaced chieftain of crime. He maintained a lavish suite in the Lexington as well as an entire floor of "business" offices and the lobby always was boiling with a swaggering pack of the pearl-gray hats.

"I've wanted to look around in there for a long time," Joe explained his suggestion. "I'd like those fine little gentlemen to know that the time has come when we'll walk right into their parlor whenever we feel like it."

"Well . . ." I commented reluctantly.

Joe grinned at me.

"You scared?"

"Yeah," I admitted slowly. "I think maybe I am. Anyhow, the prospect doesn't exactly make me feel like jumping with joy. I've got a feeling it's sort of like jailing a moonshiner without 'sightin' ' him."

Joe was puzzled.

"Now what in hell does that mean?"

"You asked for it," I told him. "You see, down in the mountains when we'd show up unexpectedly at a still, the

157

first thing those mountaineers would do was turn away,
run and never look back. They believed that if we didn't
actually see their faces we hadn't 'sighted' them. Well, you
could meet the suspect a half hour later, wearing the same
clothes and stinking of mash, but when you asked him if
he had been making likker he'd inquire 'Did you sight
anybody?' If we admitted we hadn't, meaning we didn't
see any faces of those who had escaped, they felt we had
no case. And, actually, we didn't arrest them under such
circumstances where we hadn't actually seen their faces.

"We had one agent," I went on, "who had no qualms
about claiming he had 'sighted' a violator, even if he
hadn't. Those mountain moonshiners hated him, not for
doing his duty but because he was, in their minds, a liar
who gave false testimony. Now he and I at one time both
wore black leather jackets. So one day I'm walking up a
trail and a bullet tears through my jacket, passing from the
back right between my arm and body."

"You were lucky," Joe commented.

"Damned right," I agreed. "And I really hit the dirt.
But later on, one of those mountain boys stops me in
town and says he's got a message for me from some fellow he didn't know. I knew he was speaking for himself
when he said that this other fellow asked him to tell me
that he was sorry about shooting at my black jacket and
was glad he had missed. He said the fellow was after
somebody else—and I knew he meant the agent who
swore falsely that he had 'sighted' him when he actually
hadn't."

Leeson chuckled.

"So maybe these hoods will think this 'sightin'' we're
doing is unsportsmanlike?"

"No, I guess not," I grinned. "I reckon this comes more
under the category of catching a bear by the tail."

Joe pulled reflectively at his lower lip.

"Maybe it is a lousy idea at that," he conceded.

"Too late to change your mind now," I shrugged.
"Here we are."

As I said it, I wheeled the car into the vacant loading

zone in front of the Lexington and Joe shot me a wide, reckless smile as we climbed out and headed into the lobby of the Capone headquarters.

To say that we caused a flurry of excitement is putting it mildly. There were a half-dozen hoodlums in evidence and, at a commanding nod from a stocky, sleekly handsome man in his mid-forties, three of them sidled over to one of the elevators and ranged themselves beside it in an alert, expectant manner which proclaimed that no unwelcome visitors were going to be permitted to enter this particular lift.

"The boss man there," Joe said to me in a casual aside, "is Phil D'Andrea, Capone's top bodyguard. That elevator with the watchdogs without doubt is the one which leads directly to the rat's nest upstairs."

We sauntered toward the desk and, as we approached, two hoods lounging there moved slowly away. Behind the desk, the dapper, mousey clerk to whom they had been talking in low tones drummed the counter with nervous fingers. He was white-faced and his tone disclosed his apprehension that trouble was about to explode around him.

"Yes, gentlemen," he quavered, "what can I do for you?"

Joe, leaning on his elbows, grinned down at him tauntingly.

"We just wanted to see what you charge for a suite by the week."

"I'm sorry, sir," the clerk gulped. "We are completely filled up."

"That's too bad," I interjected. "We're federal men and we have been considering the possibility of quartering all of our men here in the Lexington."

The little man looked as if he might faint at the very thought of it. His voice squeaked as he spoke hastily.

"I'm sorry, sir, but we are filled up at the moment with permanent residents and I have absolutely no idea when we might have a vacancy."

Joe turned him white on white.

"Maybe we'll take care of that sooner than anybody thinks."

We moved away from the wide-eyed clerk and noted that the two hoods who had left the desk at our approach were watching us intently from near one of those new electric pin-ball type games which at that time were just coming into vogue. This one was a pistol marksmanship affair with an electric beam making contact on each shot. A hand-lettered sign proclaimed "Twenty shots for five cents."

Strolling over to it, I slipped a nickel into the slot and squeezed off five shots. The first four were hits. The fifth missed. I let go five more. It was the same thing, a miss on the fifth attempt. Four more shots hit the bullseye but on the fifth—or fifteenth shot—I aimed a fraction high and scored a hit. Four more times I hit the bullseye and then, aiming high again on the fifth—or twentieth shot— expected a hit. But again it was a miss.

"It's rigged, and I think I know how," I explained to Joe while the two watching hoods began to idle in our direction. "I believe it has an alternate wiring gimmick in five shot sequences. Four shots and then high, four shots and then low."

Dropping in another nickel, I found it was as I suspected. Aiming high on the fifth and fifteenth shots and low on the tenth and twentieth shots, I rang up a perfect score with seeming nonchalance.

Surreptitiously, I observed the two hoods, by now standing only a few feet away, exchange surprised glances.

Then Joe dropped a nickel into the machine and, using my system, also rattled off a perfect score.

"Child's play," Joe grunted for the benefit of the watching mobsters, turning to me and adding in a voice loud enough for them to hear clearly, "Say, you know, they tell me the great Al Capone lives in this dump. I wonder what he'd say if he knew there's a sheriff in Indiana who doesn't know what a big man he is today but remembers him only as 'Al Brown, pimp and whore-house bouncer'?"

It was obvious, even to the hoods, that Joe Leeson wasn't only looking for trouble. He was begging for it. But the two simply stood there immobile and, with a sneering look in their direction, Joe suggested: "Let's get out of this stinking joint."

Unhurriedly we began moving toward the door. But I idled long enough to watch one of the hoods jam a nickel into the pistol game and chuckled as he missed those four rigged times out of his twenty shots. He muttered an oath, gave the machine a disgusted shove with his hand and followed by the other mobster moved back toward the desk.

Joe was in a particularly satisfied frame of mind when we reached the sidewalk.

"I wonder whether Al will get the message?" he mused.

I didn't think so, I told him.

"Capone, as I understand it, is very sensitive about his early career around here. It's a touchy subject and few people dare mention it in his hearing."

But, as we learned much later from an informer, D'Andrea did tell the gangster overlord of our visit and everything that we said. We were told that Scarface Al, in his rage at our effrontery, almost wrecked a whole room full of furniture.

Now, however, as we climbed into our car and I prepared to start the motor, I saw one of the mobsters emerge from the hotel and start to walk slowly up the street behind us. Getting out, I pretended to check the front tires and saw him enter a car parked a short distance away.

"I think we've picked up a tail," I told Joe. "It's my guess they wonder what this visit was all about."

"Let's take him for a little ride," Joe suggested.

We drove idly, making certain that our tail had no difficulty keeping us in view. Then I led him toward a spot where I knew there was a large billboard at the corner of an alleyway. Driving slowly until I turned the corner near the alley, I floored the gas pedal, spun the car into the al-

leyway and wheeled it out of sight behind the concealment of the billboard.

The maneuver worked perfectly. Peering through a
heavy latticework at the bottom of the billboard, we saw
the mobster pause at the alley entrance, look confusedly
in all directions and then, with a mystified shrug of his
shoulders, turn around and start back the way he had
come. We cut back through the alley, paralleled his route
for several blocks and then fell in behind him at a safe
distance. Now we were on his tail.

At this point we had another break. The mobster
parked and went into a small neighborhood candy store.
Driving past in a convoy of traffic, we saw him gesturing
while talking into a telephone.

"Reporting that he lost us," Joe hazarded.

We sped on around the block and, waiting until the
gangster reappeared, began tailing him again. It paid off
because the man drove to an apartment house on the
South Side, went inside and, after we had waited more
than an hour, reappeared wearing a different suit of
clothes.

"That's where he lives," Joe nodded. "You know, I've
got a funny feeling about this dude. Let's check him out
for a couple of days."

So it was that we "put him to bed" late that night and
were waiting when he came out the next morning.

Joe's almost mystical hunch paid off immediately.

Because we tailed the hoodlum to a warehouse and
were watching from a nearby alley when, a short time
later, he appeared riding beside the driver of a van which
quite clearly carried a heavy load.

"I'll be damned," I exulted. "We got us a brewery."

"We can take care of that tonight," Joe pointed out.
"At the moment, let's follow our little pal."

Careful not to get so close as to arouse suspicion, we
tailed the truck until it rumbled into an alley and halted
behind the Hibernian Hall. By the time we parked our car
and approached on foot, we were surprised to see a dozen

uniformed firemen helping the truck driver to unload barrels of beer and preparing to carry them into the hall.

Standing by and watching the unloading operations, the mobster we had tailed originally spotted us when we still were some distance away and he darted into the back entrance to the hall, shouting to the firemen and the truck driver as he disappeared. The rest took to their heels immediately.

"I'll get the driver," Joe barked. "You get the hood."

"Let him go," I directed on the spur of the moment. "Maybe he'll lead us to some more spots later."

Joe pounced on the driver, a round-bellied, red-faced man who had jumped out of the truck and was panting toward the rear entrance of the hall. Meanwhile, the firemen had run down to the corner of the alley and congregated there watching us.

"Okay," Joe ordered the driver, "start loading all those barrels back on the truck."

"Who me? All these barrels?" the driver protested, waving a meaty hand at what already had been unloaded. "Damned if I'm gonna load 'em."

"You'll load 'em or I'll bust 'em over your head," Joe threatened roughly.

The glowering driver took one look at Joe's muscular frame and reluctantly began to hoist the barrels back into the truck.

At about this time, a fire captain accompanied by two of his men came up the alley and approached us.

"Now look, you men," he began, "we're putting on a firemen's affair here tonight and . . ."

Leeson stared him down.

"Tough luck, captain. But this slop is illegal and we're doing the job we're supposed to be doing."

The fire captain's face turned red with indignation.

"My God, man," he argued, "I had to go all the way to the Big Boy himself to get this beer donated."

"You mean Al?" I asked.

"Sure. Al Capone. Who do you think?"

"That's just dandy," I told him. "Now you're going to come down to our office and say that where it counts."

He drew back in panic.

"Oh, no, you ain't gettin' me to say anything like that for the record. I was just talkin', that's all. You got no proof I said anything at all."

"You fat bastard," Leeson chimed in angrily. "I ought to bust you one."

"Let it go, Joe," I restrained him. "Let's just get this load the hell out of here."

The firemen watched disgustedly while the driver finished reloading and then Joe rode with him and I followed in our car while we headed for our office.

That night we gathered the squad and raided the brewery from which we had followed the truck. We hit the jackpot again for it was a big one and, from all indications, had been in operation only a short period of time. We took three more trucks and captured six prisoners who yielded without a struggle. The syndicate evidently had learned well by now that when we broke in on a raid the best thing to do was to surrender quietly.

For some time after this raid we laid off the mobster who had unwittingly led us to the brewery so as not to press our luck and make him suspicious. Then, after this cautious interval, we began another stakeout at his apartment house.

"I'll be damned if this isn't too easy," Joe grinned as, somewhat to our surprise, on the second day of our new stakeout, the hood drove to another warehouse and emerged a short time later riding as before in the cab of a large truck loaded with barrels of beer whose outlines were plainly discernible under a canvas cover.

The procedure was the same as before, albeit with a completely different format.

We tailed the truck to Cicero and followed it as it turned into an alley and pulled up behind the Hawthorne Hotel.

The Hawthorne, as we knew, was not open to the public. It was strictly a hangout for the mob, actually almost a barracks, because a great number of the hoodlums lived there and it also served as a stopping over spot for visiting members of the syndicate.

There was to be a local election the next day, as we learned later, and the mob was setting up a bar in the rear of the hotel for its strongarm election "workers."

Now, as the truck we had tailed backed up to the rear entrance and the driver swiftly began unloading, once more our approach was spotted by the mobster who, by this time, certainly must have come to regard us as his own personal nemesis.

This time he didn't wait to warn anybody, bolting into the back door of the hotel and locking it behind him.

Open mouthed, the driver stood there helplessly and, while Joe began to hurl himself against the locked door, I prodded the driver into the cab of the truck and handcuffed him to the steering post. It was the work of a second to fling open the hood and snatch loose a handful of wiring, just to make certain a confederate didn't happen along and drive off with both prisoner and load.

Quickly then I was at Joe's side and the door crashed open when we threw our combined strength against it. Ahead of us was a gloomy passageway and following it we found ourselves in the deserted kitchen of the hotel.

"This way," Joe snapped, shouldering through a pair of swinging doors into a small, empty dining room.

"There," I pointed to where an arrow was painted on the wall with the legend "Lobby" lettered in its center.

Clattering to the door, we burst out into a long, rectangular lobby and into, what I thought fleetingly, was a situation much akin to sticking a blowtorch into a beehive.

For there stood our fleeing hoodlum, talking excitedly and gesticulating expressively to five other mobsters gathered around him.

They turned at the sound of our entrance and started toward us in a body. A huge, swarthy man who obviously was the boss of this echelon strode a half pace in the lead with a fierce scowl on his ugly face. His voice was thunderously truculent.

"Whadda you guys want in here?"

Joe was just as pugnacious.

"We want that guy right there," he pointed to the man we had followed and who now was standing in the rear of the pack. "We're federal agents."

"I don't give a damn who you are," growled the massive one with the blue jowls. "Where's your search warrant?"

With this demand he rammed his chin into Joe's face and, I noted in a queerly detached manner, they were both about the same size. But it was a mistake the hood was to regret.

"Search warrant?" Joe bit off, and I could sense what was coming. "Right here."

Following up his words, Leeson hauled off and clouted the big man flush on the chin with as hard and true a punch as I'd ever had the pleasure to witness.

As if he had been poleaxed, the big man fell straight forward on his face, out cold on his feet before he hit the floor, and the lobby erupted into violent action. Because the five others surged forward and we were in the middle of a free-swinging melee, Joe's voice roaring happily above the confusion.

We had the advantage of surprise, for as Joe's man went down, I pivoted into a chunky mobster at my right, hooking a left hand to his stomach and laying him out with a followup right to the chin when my first punch doubled him over. That left it four to two and Joe momentarily reduced those odds by lifting a stiletto-thin hood completely off the floor and hurling him into two others. All three of them went down to the floor in a tangled heap.

Meanwhile, the other hood had leaped in close to me and we wrestled our way along the front of the empty hotel desk. While we were straining against each other, over his shoulder I saw that the door to the large steel hotel safe stood partially open and I caught a fragmentary glimpse of piles of ledgers and papers inside it.

My attention was painfully diverted at this point as the

mobster wrapped me in a bear hug, cutting off my breath with what seemed to be abnormally powerful arms. Lunging forward, I drove his back up against a marble column and, grabbing him by both ears, banged his head lustily against the pillar. Once, twice and he went completely limp and sagged to the floor.

Gasping for breath, I turned and leaped to Joe's assistance. He had one of the hoods in a headlock under one arm and was holding off a second with a fistful of the man's necktie, twisting it until the gangster's face was turning blue while he tore at Joe's iron grip. The little one Joe had flung at them earlier, had hurled himself onto Joe's back and wrapped both arms around Leeson's neck, trying to throttle him.

Reaching up, I grabbed him by the hair, tore him off Joe's back and swinging him around put him out of action with two quick chops to the chin. Freed of this encumbrance, Joe pulled down the head of the man he had by the necktie and simply smashed his head into the pate of the hood protruding from under his other arm. Both men dropped.

Panting, we surveyed the recumbent bodies and Joe, rubbing his hands together with wild-eyed enjoyment, looked at me and chuckled gustily.

"You got a mouse under your eye."

"And you," I told him, "have got a cut lip and a bloody nose. But we'd better get things really under control here because that safe over there behind the desk is open and it's piled high with ledgers and other stuff that should be like money from home to the Treasury Department boys."

We started for the desk, after a quick look assured us that our opponents all still were hors de combat, but then found out we weren't out of the woods yet.

Our ruckus had made quite a bit of commotion and from upstairs two more hoods came trotting down a back stairway into the lobby. Joe spun to face them and I whirled to go behind the desk when our new troubles were further complicated by two more hoods entering through the front door.

"Whatta you guys doin'?" one of those near me demanded. Then, seeing me heading for the open safe, he and his companion leaped forward and the leader bulled me away from the safe and tried to slam the door shut.

By now, however, I had experienced enough of this foolishness.

Drawing my .38, I banged the fisted butt down on the top of his head and his falling body effectively wedged open the door. Then I covered the other mobster with my pistol.

Joe had the same idea. For I heard him bark at the two who had come down the stairway, "We're federal officers. Just stand nice and quiet and nobody will get hurt. But let me warn you, this .45 makes awful big holes when it goes off."

By this time several of our original combatants were stirring. Those on their feet were lined up facing one wall. Those still recumbent, including the big man Joe had teed off on first, we dragged into the formation and dumped unceremoniously. A quick search revealed that every one of them was armed with a pistol, two of them additionally carrying knives which flipped open to menacing proportions.

"Quite an arsenal," Joe observed just as another hoodlum sauntered in from the street, was waved into line before he knew what was happening and was disarmed, too.

"I think," I told Joe, "I'd better get some help here pretty quick or we're liable to have the whole Capone mob on parade in this dump."

Joe nodded and kept the entire group under the lethal hypnotism of his .45 while I went behind the desk and telephoned the Cicero Police Department. The desk sergeant who answered took some persuading when I told him we wanted a black Mariah to take away a load of hoods from the Hawthorne.

"Did you guys have a search warrant?" he asked.

"Listen," I snapped, "we've got a load of hoods here

that are guilty of carrying concealed weapons, assault and battery, resisting arrest and, if the truth is known, probably are wanted here and any number of places on more charges than you could dream up all afternoon."

"But . . ." he started to interrupt.

I cut him off angrily.

"This is federal business. If we don't get some assistance damned quick you're going to hear howls from as far away as Washington and it's going to look pretty smelly in the newspapers."

He was surly but finally acquiescent.

"Okay, they'll be right over."

Hanging up, I then called Froelich. As rapidly as possible I explained what had happened and that Joe and I were positive there were a heap of records in the safe which would be valuable to the Treasury Department detail which was attempting to collect income tax evasion information against Capone and the mob. I told him about the obvious reluctance of the Cicero desk sergeant to send help.

"Just hang on there," Froelich told me excitedly. "It's a fine piece of work and don't worry about any repercussions. If there are any, I'll handle them. Sit tight and I'll have our squad down there immediately."

I felt relieved after talking to him because what we had done might not, in some quarters, have been regarded as strictly legal. Froelich, however, knew that we had to fight fire with fire and cut certain legal corners whenever the necessity arose.

Rejoining Joe, I saw that all of the hoods had regained their feet. They were shuffling their feet and scowling into our pistols when there was a squealing of automobile brakes out front of the hotel.

"More customers?" I wondered.

Joe simply shrugged.

But it was the Cicero police. A half dozen uniformed men under the command of a lantern-jawed captain whirled in through the front door and approached us with incredulity showing on their faces.

"Only two of you feds here?" the captain asked.

"That's all we needed," Joe told him. "But are you sure you got enough men to get 'em down to headquarters without losing any of them? We don't want any missing when we come down to file charges."

"Don't worry," the captain told us while his men herded the prisoners outside and into a patrol wagon. "There are some of us wearing uniforms who don't hold with everything that goes on around these parts. I'm one of them. Your pigeons will be in the coop when you get there."

We told him we would file charges as soon as the remainder of our squad arrived. Which wasn't long, because Froelich hadn't wasted any time briefing them and they had come to Cicero wide open.

Lahart charged through the front door followed by Chapman, the raw-boned Seager, as expressionless as ever, and the rangy, panther-like Gardner.

"Hell," Lahart grunted, "it looks like the fun's all over."

"We were in the office when you called Froelich," Chapman explained. "We made it as quickly as we could."

"You did fine," Joe grinned, "although we could have used you to better effect about a half hour or so ago."

Chapman, who always had a genius for paperwork detail, went to work immediately on the ledgers and records in the safe. He clucked his tongue and shook his head with repeated satisfaction while flipping through them.

"This is the best haul we've ever made," he approved. "The T-boys will bless you for this. Man, there are lists of deliveries, speakeasies, breweries, profits and everything else in here. This is really a gold mine of information on the gang's income."

Throughout the fracas and subsequent happenings, I had forgotten all about the truck driver I had handcuffed to the steering post of his own truck at the rear of the hotel.

"Let's give a look at the guy we left out back," I said

to Leeson, advising the others to take care of the confiscated records. Going out we found that he was still there, chafing at the long delay and with his wrist almost raw from tugging against the manacle. Speedily I fixed the loose wires on the motor and we drove him to the Cicero police station and deposited him with the others.

"A damned good day's work," I commented to Leeson as we drove back downtown.

"It's not over yet," he said. "We've still got to get the brewery we started out from."

We did too, knocking it over that night during a violent rainstorm with the full squad on hand to carry out our patented assault technique. The result was that we impounded two more trucks and a flourishing brewery operation which was so large that Barney Doyle groaned when he led his contract crew inside to put it to the axe.

"What's the matter?" Leeson asked.

"I've got a hangover," Doyle growled, "and be damned to you for makin' me work on a night like this."

It raised a laugh among us.

"That's all right," I told Doyle. "Capone will have a hangover, too, when he hears about this day's work."

"It won't make you any more popular with him," Barney predicted.

We knew that. But just how unpopular I was to learn personally not long afterwards when I barely escaped being taken for one of the mob's one-way rides.

CHAPTER 13

The south side by this time was getting to be about as wet as the Sahara and word filtered in to us that the mob, desperate for safer spots from which to run its operations, had begun crowding into the north side long controlled by "Bugs" Moran.

There was, too, a sudden difference in the manner in which the mob began to conduct its activities. It was as if an impenetrable veil of silence and secrecy had been drawn down by a giant hand. We noticed it first in the way in which our wire taps began to yield absolutely nothing. Jack Martin confirmed the new setup when he sent word to me through Mavis that he and several other collectors had been replaced without explanation and that his usual sources of information had dried up completely.

Froelich, however, had an ace hidden up his well-tailored sleeve.

I didn't know that I was it.

"The Capone mob is just beginning to infiltrate the north side rather heavily, according to information which has come to us," he briefed us at a general meeting of the squad.

Then he dropped his bomb.

"The Treasury Department unit deserves a rather large assist on this," he added, "but I believe that it is possible for us to get one of our own men in with the mob."

His plan, as he outlined it, centered around a Sicilian named Angelo Caliguri, ostensibly an olive-oil merchant on the north side but a man who actually had amassed a hidden fortune by supplying the Capone mob with a great percentage of the sugar it needed in its operations. Caliguri had attempted to keep his income secret but the Treasury Department agents had unearthed his operations and had him set up on tax evasion charges.

A devoted family man, the merchant had a son who was a student at the University of Chicago. This was his Achilles heel.

"He has volunteered to help us in hopes of lessening the scandal for his wife and, in particular, his son," Froelich explained. "We have agreed to give him the utmost consideration on condition that he cooperates with us."

"So we'll get a list of spots from him?" Leeson guessed.

"No," Froelich frowned. "Caliguri swears that he merely has the sugar delivered to his warehouse and that the mob has it picked up there. He vows that he has no knowledge concerning the location of any of the syndicate's breweries or distilleries."

"Then what good does he do us?" I interpolated.

Froelich stared at me until I began to get an uncomfortable feeling that something might be wrong with the way I was dressed. Finally he broke the silence, still looking squarely at me.

"It depends on how much good you can do us," he said.

"Me?" I said in some surprise.

"Yes. Take a look at this."

He held out something which, as I took it, I saw to be a police mug shot. The legend identified it as having come from the New York Police Department. It declared that one Harry Marble, five feet, nine inches, 170 pounds and 35 years of age, was charged with violation of the Eighteenth Amendment and the near-fatal shooting of a policeman in Brooklyn.

"So?" I asked.

Froelich smiled gently.

"Take a good look at the picture," he suggested.

I did. This Harry Marble, I mused, was a thin-faced hard-eyed character with black hair who certainly was no threat to the ladies' memories of Rudolph Valentino.

"So?" I repeated.

"Except for the black hair, it could be you," Froelich asserted.

I took another careful look and, while I never considered myself to be an Adonis, I thought ruefully that Froelich wasn't being very kind. And yet, I had to admit, the resemblance was better than most passport photos.

"I happened to be reading a New York newspaper some time back and I saw this man's picture and a story of his arrest," Froelich recounted. "I was struck immediately by his resemblance to Robsky. In reality, I sent for a copy of the mug shot to show it to Paul. But now I believe we can turn it to our benefit."

I was beginning to feel uncomfortably warm around the collar. It got warmer rapidly.

For Froelich explained that he had conferred with Caliguri and the olive oil and/or sugar merchant had agreed to introduce me to various members of the mob as "Harry Marble," a hoodlum "on the lam" from New York.

"We've made certain that Marble is to be kept on ice pending the outcome of the wounds suffered by the policeman he shot," Froelich disclosed.

"Wait just a second," I protested. "This guy has black hair and he may be known around here. Also, I'm not exactly an unknown in these parts."

Froelich had it all figured out.

"Your hair will be black, too," he smiled briefly. "A dye job will take care of that very nicely. Then we'll get you out of those dull browns and grays you usually wear, Paul, and dress you up in something snappy. We even have obtained some New York labels to be sewn in your new clothes. Frankly, when we get finished I doubt if your own mother would know you."

Fleetingly I recalled that sheriff in Indiana and took comfort from the fact that even while looking at my I.D. card he hadn't recognized me in person. It was small solace, but better than none.

"This is a highly dangerous assignment," Froelich concluded. "Will you take the chance, Paul?"

Actually, I had never even given a thought to passing it up. I was no hero, but it was part of the job I was being paid to do.

"Of course," I shrugged. "I just hope it works."

Three days later, carrying a cheap new suitcase, I mingled with the crowd in the railroad station and prepared to take a cab to Angelo Caliguri's store. I didn't know whether I felt more embarrassed at the gaudy necktie I wore, the noisy checked suit I sported or my newly blackened hair. Looking in the men's room mirror, I had to admit that I hardly knew myself.

Upon arriving at Caliguri's store on the north side, I found it to be a rather dilapidated two-story building. Angelo Caliguri was a short, gray-haired man with a round paunch and a fretful, harried manner.

"I'm Harry Marble, from New York," I told him.

Angelo nodded.

"Come, we go upstairs."

There I was in for quite a surprise. Because while the outside of the building was run down and neglected, the Caliguri apartment was truly lavish. Thick Persian rugs graced highly polished floors and heavy, opulent drapes hung at the windows. Marble figures posed artistically on pedestals and the furniture was expensive, ornately inlaid walnut.

"My wife, Rosalia," Caliguri introduced me to a plump, black-haired woman who appeared from a gleaming kitchen, turning to her and adding, "This is Mister Marble. I'm going to take him out to find a room."

"But first, Poppa," she insisted, "a cup of coffee, or maybe a glass of wine."

We had a cup of coffee and I noted the picture of a boy in his late teens standing on a sideboard. Caliguri saw me looking at it.

"My boy, Frankie," he observed proudly. "He goes to the university. He's a good boy, our Frank. Nothing must touch him."

I nodded my understanding. Caliguri was emphasizing why he was giving us his cooperation.

With Caliguri's help, I located a boarding house and obtained a room. There, as I unpacked my few new belongings, and draped a half-dozen screaming neckties in the darkest corner of the room's lone closet, we quietly made our plans.

Caliguri figured that my best chance to make a tie-in with the mob was to have him introduce me to a racketeer named Frank Moretti who made the mob's sugar payments to him. I was "Harry Marble," a hood on the "lam" from New York and a friend of Caliguri's brother, Anselmo, who lived in Brooklyn. It was hoped that such an entree would gain me invitational entrance to a pool room the mob had begun to use as one of its new north side hangouts.

It worked exactly as planned.

Moretti appeared several impatient days later and Caliguri, making some excuse to go upstairs to his apartment, called me hurriedly from there. When I arrived as speedily as possible at the store, Caliguri was just finishing his business with Moretti, a thin, cadaverous man with piercing black eyes and gleaming white teeth.

"Harry Marble, from New York," Caliguri introduced me to the mobster, lowering his voice and added confidentially, "He had a little trouble with the law in New York and he's here for a change of climate."

Brashness, I decided, was my best approach.

"What do the local yokels do for excitement around here? I'm goin' nuts with nothin' to do."

"There ain't much right now," Moretti told me. "Except for the damned feds. They're drivin' us nuts."

"I had to take care of a piece of law in New York," I boasted, patting my shoulder holster. "That's why I'm out in this dump."

Moretti was properly impressed, I could see, and, before leaving, told me to drop in at the pool room to "meet the boys."

I didn't waste any time accepting the invitation. The next afternoon I waited in a drug store across the street from the hangout until I saw Moretti enter. Then I sauntered in and found him watching a game among four of his henchmen. He beckoned me over and I could feel a cold chill skate up my spine.

One of the four had been among the mobsters who Leeson and I had knocked around when we raided the Hawthorne Hotel in Cicero.

"Say hello to Harry Marble," Moretti ordered. "He's on the lam from New York. This is Monk Molgardo . . ."

He was well-named.

". . . Cooch Curci . . ."

I wondered what the "Cooch" stood for, and never did find out.

". . . Louis Amato . . ."

Then I was face to face with the one who could bring this caper to a sudden and violent halt.

". . . and Vinnie Presco."

Presco stared at me and I could feel the hair standing up on the back of my neck. There was a puzzled frown on his narrow, saturnine face.

"Don't I know you from someplace?" he asked.

"You ever been to New York," I said, trying to harden my voice.

"No."

"You mailed any letters lately?" I grinned crookedly. "You mighta seen my kisser in the post office."

Moretti laughed.

"Yeah," he chuckled. "You musta seen Harry's phizz on a wanted poster. He blasted a cop in New York."

Presco nodded slowly but, as Moretti waved me into the back room for a drink, I saw Presco looking after me with narrowed eyes and thin lips pursed together in thought. He still wasn't quite satisfied, struggling to place me, but there was nothing I could do about it except remain vigilant and ready to beat him to a gun if it ever came to him who I really was.

But my disguise held. And in the days which followed I became a regular and accepted patron of the hangout, thanking a misspent youth for an ability to play pool which made me a welcome partner at the tables. I didn't know whether to feel flattered or not when Monk and Louie invited me to go along on a "gang bang with the best chippie in the neighborhood," avoiding participation in their romantic interlude by telling them I had another date.

This was final proof to me that I had been accepted fully and, as I expected, it wasn't long before I was being invited along for the ride when this collection and payoff crew made its rounds. Within a few more days, from observation and conversation I knew practically every speakeasy, and every beer and liquor operation in the district.

As a caution against detection, we had agreed that I shouldn't call the office until I felt I had all the information I could possibly get. Now, I figured, I had all there was to be gained and it was time to get out.

I was never more right in my life.

For when I telephoned Froelich, I could hear the agitation in his voice.

"I've been sitting here trying to decide whether to send the squad out to round you up," he said.

"What's going on?"

"Prepare yourself for a shock. The real Harry Marble broke out of jail in New York and we have it on reliable authority that he's hiding out here in Chicago. He's been out more than a week but some dolt in New York forgot to notify me."

Now I really began to sweat. They could be on to me already. I wanted out, fast, but first I had to warn Caliguri.

"I'll call him," Froelich suggested, "and offer to take him into protective custody."

"No," I held adamantly, "we owe him more than that. I'll try to bring him in."

Wasting no time, I went to Caliguri's store and, finding him and his one clerk with several customers, beckoned him aside and told him I had to see him alone at once. Paling at the urgency in my tone, he led the way upstairs. Caliguri's wife appeared from one of the bedrooms and, when he told her we wanted to be alone, she disappeared into the kitchen.

Quickly I told Caliguri about Marble's suspected appearance in Chicago.

"It's only a question of time until they find out there's two of us," I said. "Then you're going to be on the spot for introducing me. You'd better let me take you in for your own protection."

The little man refused.

"What good would it do? I think I can convince them that I knew no better. After all, you fooled them, too. How was I to blame?"

Standing at a front window and peering through the drapes, Caliguri sighed. His voice was barely audible.

"If something does happen, it is the price for breaking Omerta."

There it was, the Sicilian blood code of silence to the death.

I argued to no avail, for he remained silent, staring from the window. Then his body stiffened and his voice quavered.

"They come."

Leaping to the window where he was standing, I saw Moretti's familiar car pull up in front of the store. He got out, followed by Monk Molgardo and Cooch Curci and they made their way purposefully into the store.

Raising his voice, Caliguri called, "Mama, bring us two cups of coffee."

Then he turned to me and his tone was low but steady.

"Now listen to me and don't argue. When they come up, we are having a friendly cup of coffee. Remember this one thing, if they start talking in Italian, get out of here. I will give you an excuse, somehow."

His wife appeared from the kitchen, putting our coffee on a small table. Caliguri fondly smiled his thanks but directed her back to the kitchen with one stab of his forefinger. She went without question. Then there were footsteps on the stairs and a light tap at the door. Caliguri walked over slowly and opened it.

He was an actor.

"Ah, Signor Moretti. Come in! Come in!"

So were they.

"Hello, my good friend Angelo," Moretti beamed. "You know Monk and Cooch."

Then he spotted me. His smile was dazzling but, I conjectured, much too bright and there seemed to be a glitter in the piercing black eyes.

"Our good friend, Harry," Moretti waved, adding with an emphasis I didn't miss, "from New York."

We might all have been fraternity brothers, so hearty were the greetings. However, Caliguri was busily plotting my exit.

"A glass of wine," he suggested.

Moretti protested that they had only dropped in for a moment but Caliguri ignored him and bustled into the kitchen, returning almost immediately with a bottle of wine that was less than half full. Briskly he went to the sideboard, returned with five glasses and poured equal shares into them until the bottle was empty.

"Long life," Moretti toasted sardonically, sipping a little of the wine and then, setting his glass down carefully, turning to Caliguri. He had, he said, some private business to transact.

"Forgive me," Moretti shot me that wolfish smile.

Then he began to speak rapidly in Italian!

Caliguri's eyes widened dramatically. Then he held up a protesting hand, drained his glass and turned to me.

"Harry, that is all the wine I have up here. Will you step down to the store and tell Luigi to give you another bottle?"

It was my cue to head for the tall timber. I was suspect.

"Oh, no," Moretti burst forth, "we have no time."

"Nonsense," Caliguri insisted. "Harry will get the bottle."

It was less than twenty feet to the door but it felt like a mile—the last mile. Then the door closed behind me and I was down the stairs and out in the air.

But I couldn't leave Caliguri in the lurch.

Staying close to the building so that I couldn't be seen from the windows above, I ducked into the store. There were no customers and Luigi, the clerk, was busy in the back. I stepped into a niche behind a pile of boxes and checked my .38. If there was any blasting upstairs, there was going to be some down here, too. Nor, I resolved, would I let them take Caliguri away in their car.

For fifteen nervous minutes I sweated it out. Then I tensed at the muffled tread of footsteps from above. But, a cautious peek showed me, the three hoods didn't have Caliguri in tow and they went directly to their car and drove off. When they had disappeared from view, Caliguri came down into the store.

"It is as I thought," he murmured, looking to make certain that his clerk was out of earshot. "They have you pegged as a phony but they aren't quite sure who you are. I told them you were obviously an imposter because you didn't come back with the wine and quite apparently had run away. I think they believed me when I said I was astonished and I took some credit for exposing you in this manner. Now, you had better disappear."

"And you?"

"I think it will be all right. But if they do want me, your jails would not keep me safe."

I shook hands with the little man and gave him my name and phone number. Then I walked through to the rear of the store, cut through several alleys and made my way to a drug store. Calling Froelich, I told him of the developments and he told me to stay where I was until Leeson picked me up.

Joe made good time and, as I went out and got into the car with a gusty sigh of relief that this masquerade was ended, he grabbed my hand in a crushing grip and greeted me with a wide smile.

"Hello, 'Harry,' my little sitting duck. Welcome home."

"The first thing I want to do," I told him distastefully, "is get rid of these clothes."

Meanwhile, we knew that we had to move fast, now

that I had been uncovered as an imposter, and seldom if ever was the mob struck with such a crippling blow as we now delivered. Swooping down on the north side with a list of mob operations I had been able to compile, we knocked over three large breweries, four mammoth alcohol plants and an even dozen speakeasies in the course of three days and nights of frenzied action.

"Dammit," Barney Doyle complained as we summoned his contract wrecking crew from one spot to another almost without surcease, "I didn't expect to have to work twenty-four hours a day, seven days a week on this lousy job."

The mob, as might have been expected, didn't take it lying down. Their law always had been an eye for an eye and a tooth for a tooth. Somebody had to pay for what had happened.

It was Angelo Caliguri.

His wife was sobbing and almost incoherent when she telephoned me.

"My Angelo, he tell me to call you, Mister Robsky, right away if anything bad happen to him," she wailed, and I knew that Caliguri had suspected his excuses would be to no avail. "I call you now. My Angelo, he is dead."

Somewhere in the back of my mind I must have expected this. Yet, for a moment, I was stunned by this swift, deadly retribution.

"I'll be right there," I told her.

"What kind of help can I give her," I said bitterly to Joe after I picked him up and we sped to the Caliguri home.

Angelo was, indeed, quite dead. He lay on one of those thick Persian rugs of which he had been so proud. Under his head was a pillow. In his head were four bullet holes.

"Mister Marble . . .?" Mrs. Caliguri hesitated.

"No," I corrected gently. "I'm really Paul Robsky of the Prohibition Bureau. Angelo was helping us. He was a brave man."

"What good?" she cried.

"He wanted your Frankie to be proud of him," I tried to comfort her. "But tell me, what happened?"

"Those three who were here and another with a thin, sly face," she said, and I knew the last one had been Vinnie Presco, the one from the Hawthorne Hotel. "They came. They drank wine. They were telling the stories and I could hear them laughing from where I sit in the kitchen. Then there are shots. I run in. My Angelo is there."

Tears running down her face, she pointed to Angelo's body.

"Who put the pillow under his head?" I questioned.

"The one with the white smile," she recalled. "As I come in, he puts the pillow, very gently, and fires a gun into Angelo's head."

That would be Moretti, I knew. It was he who had administered the Mafia *coup de grace*.

The police came in and I took Mrs. Caliguri into the kitchen.

"I want you to identify these men," I told her.

A hooded look dropped over her face. Straightening her shoulders and drying her eyes, she shook her head slowly.

"No. It will do no good. I do not know them. Besides, there is our Frankie to think about."

No argument that I could summon was able to make her change her mind. Again it was Omerta, the Sicilian law of silence beyond death.

But, identification or not, I knew who they were. And, I told Leeson with an icy rage building inside of me, I meant to make them pay for killing the little man.

"Maybe it won't be strictly legal," I grunted. "But there will be no kickbacks."

Joe's teeth snapped together like those of a hungry alligator.

"Lay it out, Paul. Whatever you say."

I knew where they were to be found. I had been in that pool room too many times as one of their own killing kind.

They usually left their hangout at about nine o'clock each night for whatever happened to be their business of the evening, and we staked out the pool room, sitting in our car just a few doors away. The first night, they left separately. That wasn't what I wanted. I needed them all together.

On the third night, it fell the way I wanted it. For Moretti came out followed by the aptly-named Monk, the favor-currying Cooch and the weasel-faced Presco. Leaping from the car, I ran around the front and called loudly.

"Hey, Moretti, come over here. I want to talk to you."

Stiff-legged, Moretti swaggered toward me, followed by the other three. Then, as he came near me, he recognized who I was.

Moretti smiled ghoulishly, tongue licking out over those long white teeth.

"Well, well, if it ain't our old pal Harry Marble. We been lookin' for you, Harry."

Anger rose within me until I could scarcely breathe.

"And we been looking for you for the murder of Angelo Caliguri," I snapped back.

"Get him," Moretti barked his order at the three other hoodlums while his hand lanced toward his shoulder holster.

The night exploded.

Moretti's first shot spanked into the radiator of our car, inches away from my head as I dropped to one knee and in the same motion dug out my .38. Sighting carefully, I squeezed the trigger and Moretti pitched face forward, his convulsive movements triggering two more shots into the ground.

The three other mobsters had their guns out and were blasting wildly. I sighted on Presco as the chattering thunder of Leeson's tommygun erupted from the front window of our car. Presco jerked upright on his toes as I snapped a shot into him and then all three of them wilted to the ground under the garden hose stream of lead with which Joe sprayed them.

It was over in a few seconds.

All four of them had paid for the life of Angelo Caliguri, who knowingly sacrificed his life to save his wife and son from scandal.

CHAPTER 14

The whole Chicago situation began to shape up to a smashing conclusion early in 1931. It was an open secret that information concerning Capone and his henchmen soon was to be presented to the grand jury and, while Scarface Al boasted openly that the panel wouldn't be able to touch him, there was a growing feeling as a result of our juggernaut activities that the mob's days were numbered.

My own relationship with Mavis also was coming to a head.

One morning when we were having breakfast in her apartment she smiled tentatively at me and there was a hopeful note in her voice as, without preamble, she asked:

"Paul, don't you ever think that maybe we should make this arrangement legal?"

I almost choked over the coffee I was swallowing. Placing my cup down carefully, I tried to figure out how best to answer as I looked across the table at her.

There was no question in my mind but that Mavis, sitting there in a filmy negligee, was a beautiful as well as a desirable woman. Her russet hair curled softly around her face. The golden-brown eyes looked at me with doe-like trust and gentleness. We experienced, I confessed to myself, a comforting and mutually satisfactory partnership whenever we were together.

But, I wondered as I toyed absent-mindedly with a spoon, how do you tell a woman that, through some strange alchemy, you aren't in love with her to the point of always and forever. Some elusive element on which I couldn't quite put a finger, but which I always had considered necessary to marriage, was, somehow, missing from our relationship despite the powerful affection in which I held her.

"It isn't that you don't mean a great deal to me," I stammered. "Damn it, you do, and you know it. But, well, on the job I'm doing, Mavis, marriage is a damned risky business. You never know, from one day to the next, whether you'll be coming home the next time you walk out the door and . . ."

Mavis smiled tenderly, rose impetuously and coming around the tiny table in the brightly painted breakfast nook, took my head between her soft hands and halted my monologue with a compassionate kiss.

"It's all right," she hushed me with a slight catch in her voice, straightening and pulling my head close against the lacy fragrance of her bosom so that I couldn't see her face. "I understand. You don't have to make excuses, Paul, really you don't."

Dabbing furtively at her eyes, Mavis returned to her chair and when I looked at her once more she was smiling brightly as if nothing untoward had happened. Her voice was lilting again.

"I just wanted to make certain how you felt, Paul," she explained. "You see, I've had a marriage proposal from an old beau and, well, I've just about gotten the big city out of my blood and security and my own home is beginning to look pretty enticing to me. I won't pretend, though, that you don't come first."

Haltingly she told me about it. An old boy friend from her home town back in Iowa had arrived in Chicago on a business trip and had looked her up.

"He's truly nice and he's also very successful," Mavis related. "Oh, nothing has happened between us yet, not the way that look on your face insinuates, anyhow. But he wants me to marry him and go back home."

She paused and reached across the table and patted my hand.

"I had to know how you felt and now I know. I'm sorry, Paul, but I'm a big girl and I think I understand what it is you're trying to say. I do want you to know though, that I'll take some wonderful memories with me if I do go."

"Security must be a wonderful thing," I agreed cautiously. "I'm just guessing, however, because I've never had much of it and don't know if I ever will. In this job it's one crisis after another; one new town after another. It would be a helluva life for a wife."

It was lame, but it was the best I could do on the spur of the moment.

"There's one other thing that has been really worrying me," Mavis frowned prettily. "If I leave Chicago, what will happen to Jack? I know he won't be safe here because with him it's always out of the frying pan into the fire. And I doubt very much if I can influence him to go with me, even though Herbert has offered to give him a good job."

"Herbert, huh?"

"Yes," she tittered at my interruption. "Herbert Holtzbauer, and he's a very successful contractor and a very eligible bachelor, which is more than I can say for some others I happen to know."

"Nice name," I gulped, not wanting to get pinned in a corner again, and then returned hastily to the subject of her brother. "Look, I could keep an eye on Jack for you. It's the least I could do."

But within a month, in which I saw less and less of Mavis and during which time she told me that she finally had accepted Holtzbauer's proposal of marriage, the matter was taken completely out of our hands.

Holtzbauer had returned happily to Iowa, carrying with him Mavis' promise that she would join him as soon as possible, when she called me one afternoon. I was in my apartment, quite fortunately as it developed, and Leeson and I were just preparing to leave.

"I'm so glad I found you at home, Paul," Mavis said

rantically. "I'm quite certain that Jack is in terrible trou-
le."

She had arranged a late luncheon date with him at the
Vallington Hotel, she explained, planning to plead with
im one final time to return to Iowa and accept an honest
ob from his future brother-in-law. But when she arrived
n the lobby where she was to meet him, Jack was sitting
n a couch between two men. Almost imperceptibly he
ad shaken his head at her and then turned his eyes in
nother direction. Mavis had walked slowly past him and
nade some innocuous inquiry at the desk. Then she
nobtrusively entered a telephone booth and called me.

"The two men are absolutely menacing," Mavis said
ith her voice atremble. "They aren't talking and Jack
eems to be petrified. I have a feeling that they are wait-
ng for someone, but for whom or what I can't imagine."

I could. Quite obviously, from her description of their
ctions, the mob at long last had caught up to Jack Mar-
n, informer. Unless something was done, and quickly,
Iavis' brother unquestionably was destined for one of
nose one-way rides in which the mob specialized.

"Sit tight," I ordered. "We'll be right over."

Ten minutes later, during which time I explained the
etails to Leeson while enroute, we walked into the lobby
f the Wallington, a small, middle-class hotel with a
eighborhood reputation for an excellent cuisine. One
weeping glance showed me Mavis fidgeting in a chair at
ne end of the lobby, nervously twisting a tiny handker-
hief in her hands, and her brother still immobile between
vo hoodlums on a couch not far from the front door.
Iavis started to rise but I waved to her to stay where she
as. I didn't want her in the way of any harm if this thing
eveloped into open trouble.

Jack's handsome face was pale but it lighted up like a
hristmas tree when he saw Leeson and me swing toward
im. Joe brushed past a potted palm and took his station
ehind the couch. I stepped up facing the three men,
ho were sitting low and deep in its broken-spring,
ather-armed embrace.

"Hi, Jack," I greeted Martin, meanwhile ignoring th
two others. "Sorry I'm late for lunch. You ready?"

Jack made a motion as if to rise but one of the other
laid a detaining hand on his arm. The hoodlum's voic
was surly.

"He's decided to have lunch with us."

I grinned down at him.

"Listen, Buster, you look to me as if you eat too much
anyhow, so skipping this one meal doesn't figure to hur
you a bit. Now, if you've got any more objections, mak
your move. But I'd suggest you consider all the angle
first, like, say, right behind you."

Both hoods swiveled their heads and carefully eye
Joe's massive form towering behind them. Leeson wa
grinning thinly and his crossed arms showed plainly tha
his right hand was under his coat and on the butt of hi
shoulder-holstered pistol. Neither man said anything els
but both were glowering vindictively as I reached down
caught Jack by the hand and hoisted him up from th
couch.

"Let's go," I directed, leading Martin toward the fror
door and motioning Mavis to join us.

Leeson waited until we were safely on our way an
then followed along.

"Phew," Mavis' handsome brother expelled gustil
pulling out a handkerchief and mopping his forehea
"That was close. Those bastards grabbed me right the
in the lobby and phoned for a car to come pick us u
They told me they had found out I was working with th
feds and promised in no uncertain terms that I was goir
to be paid in full."

Then anger clouded his face.

"And you guys, you're a pack of bastards, too. Som
how they got hold of a report I mailed to Froelich one
those times I couldn't contact you personally."

I cut him off with a show of irritation. This was a goc
spot to drive home the point that he was finished in Ch
cago.

"You didn't think you were getting a hundred bucks

week to play with paper dolls, did you?" I rode him savagely. "But I'll tell you one thing, sonny, you're washed up in this town. Right this minute you're lucky you're not lying in a gutter somewhere with even more holes in your head than you've got, or maybe scraping the bottom of the lake in a concrete overcoat."

"Maybe he'll make it yet," Joe growled as he joined us outside just in time to hear what I had said to Martin. "Give a look."

Leeson gestured with his head toward a car which pulled into the curb in front of the hotel. The two men in the front seat had the standard earmarks of mob hoodlums. Martin shrank back behind us but Joe didn't waste any time. He strode forward and, leaning down with his big hands gripping the side of the car, looked contemptuously at the two occupants.

"You're a little late," he snarled. "Sorry to spoil your party but now you'd better get your asses moving out of here. And if I find you crummy bastards tailing us, you'll wish to hell you'd never seen the light of day."

There was no argument from the hoods. The one who was driving slammed the car into gear and it rocketed away.

Deciding to go back to my apartment, we were extremely cautious. Joe took a roundabout route with me checking constantly against our having picked up a tail. Eventually we were satisfied that no one was behind us. They quite apparently had taken Leeson at his word.

Mavis, sitting in the back seat with me, whispered her gratitude while we drove toward my place.

"I'm all ready to leave, all packed," she said, looking at me as if to ask once again if this really was what I wanted.

"Fine," I nodded. "I think you're doing the smart thing, honey. But now we have to figure out how to get you and your brother both out of town safely without running into a firing squad."

We decided that it even was too risky for Jack to go back to his hotel for his clothes and that they would have

to be left behind. Being something of a dandy, he protest
ed. But he weakened rapidly when we pointed out that i
would be an invitation to disaster and, for once, restrainec
his impulsiveness and agreed it was the best plan.

I had been contemplating a visit to my folks in Gales
burg the next day and, leaving nothing to chance in th
face of the underworld's vengeful retribution, we arrangec
for Joe to obtain another car and tail us out of Chicago.

The next morning, after spending the night in my now
somewhat crowded quarters, we stopped briefly at Mavis
apartment to pick up her baggage and with Joe wheelin;
along behind us as a rear guard headed out on a roac
parallel to the route I usually used in going to Galesburg
There was, a few miles out, a seldom-used dirt road cuto!
which I knew led across country and joined the highway
ordinarily traveled home.

When we reached it, I turned in and waved to Joe
Gradually he fell behind, making certain that nobody wa
behind us or would overtake us. As we had plotted, half
way across this road he planned to have "motor trouble
in such a way as to effectively block it, and I knew tha
no one was going to get past him until we were long gon
on our way. Once we were safely started, Joe was to re
turn to Chicago.

Our plan worked without incident and we made th
trip silently, each of us busy with our individual thought;
And, after we arrived in Galesburg, I left Mavis and he
brother at my parents' home and went out and bought
second hand car from a long-time friend who ran a ga
rage. Despite my mother's insistence, they decided not t
spend the night. Galesburg promised to be much to
prosaic for the gregarious Jack and Mavis, now that ou
parting was at hand, seemed anxious to make the brea
as swiftly as possible.

"See you around," the irrepressible Jack quipped as I
shook hands and impatiently started the motor. "Thank
for everything."

Mavis stood there woodenly, tears bubbling in thos

golden brown eyes. Reaching out, I took her in my arms right in front of my folks and kissed her tenderly.

"Goodbye, baby," I whispered. "The best of everything and I hope it all turns out the way you want it to be."

Clinging fiercely, her arms laced around my neck, she crushed her mouth against mine again. Then, turning suddenly and jumping into the car, she dried her eyes hastily and gave me that familiar dazzling smile.

"Goodbye, Paul. I wish it could have been different."

I stood there looking after them silently as the car roared away. There was a tug at my arm and my mother's voice was soft.

"Somebody special, Paul?"

"No, Mom," I forced a smile and put an arm around her as we started into the house. "You're my girl."

I don't think it fooled her. Mothers have a way of knowing when there is an aching emptiness in your heart. And it was as sure as Al Capone and income taxes that I was going to miss Mavis Martin even more than I could imagine.

Not long afterwards, back in Chicago, I received in the mail one of those printed wedding announcements which proclaimed that Miss Mavis Martin and Mister Herbert Holtzbauer had been married and would be "at home" after such and such a date. Reading it made me feel a wave of melancholy but, I reasoned with myself, Mavis now at least had the security she wanted so desperately.

My male vanity recovered quickly, however, when shortly thereafter there was a letter from Mavis in my mail box. Her new husband, she wrote, was kindly and solicitous and they had a nice home which was everything he had pictured.

But it was the postscript which, a man's pride being what it is, set me to laughing. It said:

P.S.: I shouldn't say this, but you're still the best man I ever knew, in or out of bed.

As ever,
Mavis.

Fondly I thought reminiscently of that first night we were together, after Leeson and I had been almost fatally ambushed and I had gone to her apartment, and how she blushingly had said this very same thing the next morning.

"Damn," I reminded myself aloud while placing the letter carefully in my pocket. "I never did remember to tell her about old man Austin and the bull."

Chicago was, for me, a rather dull place for a while with Mavis gone and our raids falling off simply because we had just about dried up the whole area. However, some of the restlessness was worn off as our days became even longer than usual, because now we were spreading our search operations to outlying communities; rural towns and isolated farms to which the mob had been driven in an attempt to maintain its vanishing beer and alcohol supply.

A bombshell exploded in June of 1931 when the grand jury, refuting Capone's boasts, returned indictments against the scarfaced leader of the mob and sixty-eight others for a total of five thousand violations of the prohibition law. Capone also was indicted for failure to pay $215,000 in taxes on an income of $1,050,000 from 1924 through 1929.

In retrospect it was a skeletal estimate, at that. Because Capone, who immediately went free again after posting bail of $50,000, offered haughtily to settle the income tax charge by paying $4,000,000 in interest and penalties.

Meanwhile, the gangland overlord predicted openly that he would get off with a minimum of two and a half years in prison. Actually, he tentatively had been promised a deal if he would plead guilty.

So I felt like cheering out loud when in July, one month after the indictments were returned, Capone appeared before Federal Judge James H. Wilkerson and was told with a stern and utter finality that there would be "no bargaining" in his court. Capone, realizing that Wilkerson intended to throw the book at him, withdrew his plea and trial was set for October.

The intervening weeks promised to be a further period

of inactivity, with the mob walking softly and holding itself inconspicuously quiet, but I wasn't destined to find it so. For, because of my flying experience, I was drafted to handle an out of town undercover assignment which provided me with all the excitement I needed during the interim.

CHAPTER 15

My hazardous and yet welcome interlude began when Froelich summoned me to his office and said that he had a request for special assistance from the New Orleans office.

"There doesn't seem to be too much stirring around here at the moment and, going through the records in Washington in a search for the right man to handle their job, they discovered that you're a flyer from away back," Froelich explained.

Interested, I leaned forward in my chair.

"They've asked for you," he informed me. "Now, we can spare you for the time being. The question is, do you feel like leaving here and going to New Orleans long enough to help track down what they believe is a tremendously widespread liquor smuggling ring?"

"Let me at it," I grinned. "This town is so quiet it's starting to give me the heebie-jeebies."

The next thing I knew I was on the crack express train from Chicago to New Orleans, with orders to report to the Assistant U.S. Attorney. And, relaxing in the almost vacant diner, I realized with a start how deeply I had been immersed in my work. For it wasn't until now, with hardly any passengers on the whole train, that it came to me how desperate was the depression in which the nation was wallowing.

Upon arriving in New Orleans I reported immediately to the office of the Assistant United States Attorney, a surprisingly young man named James McDaniels who was a breezy, college-athlete type, well dressed and springy of step.

He filled me in rapidly on the job at hand.

There was, he told me, a private flying service operated in New Orleans by one Harry Carling, an Englishman who had been a flying officer in the Royal Air Corps. Carling, McDaniels related, was barely eking out an existence with his four-passenger Stinson, a plane which was equipped with pontoons. A few weeks earlier, he had been flying a man and his wife to a small island off the coast when he had to make an emergency landing. Gliding in, he had managed to set the plane down without incident but then it had struck a submerged object and rammed a hole in one of the pontoons. The ship nosed over but remained afloat and Carling and his two passengers, none of whom had been injured, crawled out and clung to the buoyant plane.

"Then came the catch, as far as Carling was concerned," said McDaniels. "He had set the plane down not far from a Coast Guard station and yet he hadn't been sighted. None of the three were good swimmers and the water was too deep and it was just a bit too far to shore for any of them to risk trying to make land. They tried calling for help but there was no sign of observation from the Coast Guard station and they stayed there for several hours, holding on to the floating fuselage, until a private boat happened along and took them off."

Carling, according to McDaniels, had been furious at the men in the station whose duty it was to be alert for persons in distress. Angrily, the flyer had written a scorching letter of denunciation to the station, advising the officer in charge that he intended to carry his complaint to Coast Guard headquarters in Washington.

"Shortly thereafter," McDaniels recounted precisely, "a chief petty officer named Roy Ellingsworth, who in some manner had intercepted the letter, paid Carling a visit at his charter office. The upshot of his visit was that he told Carling he was in line for promotion, that he had been in charge of the station at the time of the accident, and that if Carling reported to Washington he, Ellingsworth, would not only lose his promotion but possibly face demotion as well."

The C.P.O. had offered Carling $500 in cash to forget the whole incident. Carling admitted that he was short of cash and, having cooled off to some extent as well as being reluctant to spoil a man's chances for promotion, he had accepted the money.

Ellingsworth then decided to capitalize on Carling's lack of funds, McDaniels declared. The chief petty officer had advanced his proposition boldly.

"There's a lot of money to be made on the side," the C.P.O. told Carling. "In my position, I'm quite often able to look the other way while certain goods are brought ashore from ocean-going vessels by small boat. But this is getting more and more risky. Besides, it takes up a good deal of time."

Carling pretended interest in the possibility of making some quick money.

"Now," Ellingsworth had suggested, thinking he had Carling hooked at the prospects of easy profits, "if we had a plane, one like yours with pontoons on it, we could meet any vessel well outside and fly the cargo inland to a safe destination."

The C.P.O's fatal mistake was in thinking that the Briton would do almost anything in his need for money. He overlooked the fact that Carling, as a former officer and gentleman, still lived rigidly by those tenets in which he had been so well indoctrinated.

"Carling pretended to accept the scheme but claimed that he needed time for two reasons," the Assistant United States Attorney elucidated. "He told Ellingsworth that he required an inestimable period to make necessary repairs to his plane and that, in no case, could he cooperate in such a scheme until his partner returned from a trip he had made."

"His partner?" I asked.

"Yes," McDaniels smiled jauntily. "You!"

"That was why you needed an agent who could fly," I guessed.

"Right," the young lawyer agreed. "Carling came to us with the whole story but, he figured rightly, he would need someone along to make seizures or arrests, if and when the time came. So he had to have a reason that wouldn't make Ellingsworth suspicious for having someone flying with him. It was a bit of quick thinking on his part. Good man. So that's where you came in. We had to have an agent who could fly, if necessary, or at least know enough about airplanes to avert any suspicion. I've been over your record, an excellent one by the way, and you fill the bill admirably."

This young man was so glowingly exuberant that I felt as if I should curtsey, or something.

But I had to admit that he did have his plan figured out in fool-proof fashion.

"We have reason to feel in these days of excessive graft and corruption that no public official is completely honest unless proved otherwise," McDaniels asserted. "It's merely a happenstance of the times, as I suppose you know. But no one is to know that you are a federal agent while you are on this assignment; not the police nor even the district prohibition agents."

McDaniels insisted that I leave every bit of personal identification with him and suggested that I rig myself out in something "more fitting to a dashing flyer" than the plain brown business suit which I was wearing.

"Your cover-up name while you are here will be 'Paul Roberts' and if by any chance you should need to contact me, I am listed in the telephone book," he directed, handing me a set of car keys and a slip of paper with an address lettered on it in precise script. "Now, here is Carling's address and you will find a red roadster parked out in back of the building for your use while you are on this assignment."

McDaniels rose briskly and held out his hand.

"And now, 'Paul Roberts,'" he said like Teddy Roosevelt at the bottom of San Juan Hill, "you are on your own. The best of luck."

Shutting the door behind me, I exhaled gustily. That McDaniels "plumb wore me out listening," as old man Austin used to say of the few fast talkers we had back in South Carolina.

Yet there was no questioning the neatness of his plan or the efficiency of his preparations. And, as he had suggested, even before locating a hotel room I stopped in a second-hand store and bought something "more fitting to a dashing flyer" than the clothes I had brought with me.

My purchases consisted of a brown leather jacket, several army-style khaki shirts, flared riding breeches, a white silk scarf to be worn Ascot fashion and, after quite a search, a pair of leather riding boots, well worn so as not to betray their recent acquisition but still in serviceable condition.

Such a getup was, in the '30's, considered the ideal costume for a flyer. Still, after my long usage of prosaic everyday wear, I felt a little as if I was getting ready to double for Douglas Fairbanks in some screen epic about the Lafayette Escadrille.

Carling, when I drove up to his river hangar, took no notice whatsoever of my attire but accepted it as strictly *de rigueur*, a lack of reaction which made me wonder if maybe I wasn't getting kind of stodgy myself.

The Englishman was a tall, spare, bony-shouldered man with white-blond hair, a wisp of a moustache and the bluest eyes I'd ever seen. His plane perched on a sliding ramp at the river's edge and when I arrived he was absorbed in carefully applying a water repellent to its pontoons. Seeing me, he laid down the brush and stretched his cramped back muscles as I introduced myself.

"I'm Paul Roberts. The plane looks in fine shape."

"Delighted, old boy," he said in a clipped voice, wiping his hand carefully on a rag and shaking mine with easy strength. "I've been expecting you. Yes, she's shipshape now."

I liked him immediately; for his easy manner, his already proven honesty and for the fond manner in which he rubbed the fuselage of his Stinson, almost as if it was a human being. We got along famously from the start.

Sitting in the shade of a wing, Carling and I went over once again everything that McDaniels had told me. But, Carling added, not knowing just when I would appear on the scene he seemingly had stalled too well.

"I told Ellingsworth that we couldn't possibly be ready for business for at least another week," he frowned. "So we'll have to wait several more days before I ring up the chap or he might become suspicious, what?"

There was no sense in unduly rushing things, I agreed. In the first place he was right about not seeming to be in too much of a hurry. In the second place, I hadn't been in New Orleans for some time and I figured that a couple of nights looking over the town again would provide a welcome respite.

This was a Tuesday and we laid plans for Carling to call Ellingsworth and set up a date for Friday afternoon at the hangar. Then, as I prepared to leave, I stopped and turned to the Englishman.

"Say, Harry," I asked, "are there any decent 'speaks' in town where a man can get a drink that won't ruin his stomach?"

He grinned delightedly.

"Tell me, old fellow, is this business for you or are you merely out to relax a bit along with the remainder of your law-breaking citizenry?"

"Just a lonesome law-breaker," I chuckled.

Carling relished the thought.

"In that case, a chap I know operates a spot just a bit off Rampart Street, and if you tell him I sent you, he'll take jolly good care of you. But I do hope you're playing cricket with me. Matter of fact, I'd like to step out a bit with you but I'm afraid the old girl might object."

The "old girl," when I met his wife, was a bright-eyed gamin some ten years Carling's junior. I didn't blame him for preferring to stay home.

That night I visited the "speak" which Carling had

recommended, a cellar establishment in the French Quarter, and laying duty aside for the time being enjoyed a few drinks. I also enjoyed the company, because it was there I met Celeste, a statuesque young lady of the evening with shameless morals and the soul of a saint. Not even the years have been able to dim my memory of her alabaster beauty, the fragrance of her shoulder-length black hair or the sweetness of her Mona Lisa smile.

"Buy a drink?" she asked, pausing at the table at which I was sitting.

"Why not?"

Over a period of several hours we talked. She told me of her childhood years in the bayou country and of her compulsive yearning to come to New Orleans. At closing time I was reluctant to leave her.

"I will go to your hotel with you for ten dollars and spend the night," she offered.

"Sorry," I told her. "I'm busted. These drinks used up most of my money and I've only got a few dollars left."

She patted my hand and twined her arm through mine.

"I like you. I will go with you for nothing."

She did. And it became a routine through my nights in New Orleans.

They threatened to stretch into quite some time, too, because Carling advised me that Ellingsworth was on sea duty and our meeting would have to be postponed until his return early the following week.

The waiting was painless, with Celeste there to occupy my spare time. But when there was another delay in meeting Ellingsworth early the following week, I decided I had better send Froelich a wire. So, accompanied by the Englishman, I drove along Canal Street and, parking in front of a bank across the street from the Western Union office, strolled over to the telegraph office. My message to Froelich in Chicago, I admitted later to myself, was somewhat cryptically condemning.

"Job tougher than I thought," I wrote it out. "Will crack it in time to be back for the big blowout."

I merely wanted to inform him that I planned to finish

up this assignment in time to be on hand for the Capone trial.

Paying for the wire, I noticed a ponderous man with "policeman" written all over him step to the counter as I walked away but gave it absolutely no thought.

It came back to me like a ton of bricks when I stepped into the roadster and had barely turned to talk to Carling when two uniformed policemen raced up with drawn guns and leaped onto the runningboard. The plainsclothesman I had automatically noted in the telegraph office was right behind them. Their voices were harshly commanding.

"You're under arrest. Get 'em up."

Too surprised to protest, I submitted to an order to get out of the car and quite a crowd gathered as they frisked us.

"Looks like we got the right ones," the plainclothesman observed loudly as he tugged the .38 from my hip pocket. "Some of Capone's hoods. I've got the wire right here."

He waved my telegram in evidence.

Almost forgetting my instructions, unconsciously I started to identify myself as a federal agent. Then I remembered that I was only "Paul Roberts, potential smuggler," and clamped my lips together.

Roughly we were hauled to the precinct house, stripped of our effects, which in my case were very few, and tossed into a cell. We were suspected, it seemed, of being a couple of bank robbers for whom the police had a pickup bulletin and had been "caught in the act" in casing the bank in front of which I had parked.

But I didn't intend to spend the night in the "tank," already occupied by a half-dozen evil-smelling drunks and vagrants.

"Hey," I called to the turnkey. "I know damned well I'm entitled to one telephone call, and I insist on making it or somebody's going to catch hell."

It required some persuasion but finally I was taken to the desk and allowed to make my call. McDaniels was in his office and, cupping one hand around the mouthpiece so I wouldn't be overheard, I told him of our plight.

Within a half hour we were out of there.

"I say, old chap," Carling raised his eyebrows at me in amusement, "you must indeed be a very desperate character."

"Maybe it's because I was associating with you," I grinned back.

Celeste found it very humorous, too, when that night I told her what had transpired.

"It will happen to me sometime, I suppose," she shrugged philosophically. "But as yet I have never been in a jail."

Often, in the years that followed, I have wondered whether she ever made it.

The very next day, remembering that my wire apparently had not gone off but had been seized by the plainclothesman, I picked up Carling and once again we drove back to the Western Union office.

"I say," Carling smiled wryly, "it couldn't possibly happen to us again, could it?"

I didn't think so, either. But damned if it didn't.

This time I had waited inside until my wire went off. But, as I returned to the car the same plainclothesman appeared, accompanied this time by his partner. He looked surprised when he recognized us and walked over belligerently.

"Just who are you guys?" he demanded curtly.

Carling quietly pulled out his wallet to display his identification but I wise-cracked to the detective: "Oh, hell, we beat that rap yesterday."

"Let's see some identification, wise guy," he directed.

McDaniels had mine. I was empty.

"Okay, okay," the detective grunted, "let's see if you can beat a vagrancy rap."

And there we were, back in the same station house and the same tank with the same half-dozen boozers.

"Somebody around here is in a rut," I yelled at the turnkey of the day before.

"Maybe it's us," Carling chuckled with infallible good humor.

We went through the identical process as previously. I made a call to McDaniels and a half hour later we were out. The breezy young attorney thought it was quite funny. I thought it was a nuisance and determined to stay out of the mid-city area until my work was finished.

The job shaped up quickly when Ellingsworth appeared on the scene and Carling summoned me to a meeting at his hangar. Without hesitation, I was accepted as Carling's partner by the chief petty officer, a burly, powerfully muscled man whose weather-beaten features attested to his calling.

"Is it a deal?" he asked Carling without wasting any time.

"Let's hear your proposition," I interjected.

Ellingsworth turned to me and nodded.

"There's a freighter, the Alhambra, which will be laying to about fifteen miles due south in the gulf the day after tomorrow. You set down next to it and the captain will put aboard your cargo."

Again I interrupted; assuming that he was talking about a load of liquor.

"We may have a problem with the weight," I protested. "What do you think the load will come to?"

Ellingsworth grinned at me.

"Don't worry about weight. You'll only be carrying a tin about the size of a brick at the end and about two feet long. That one little sealed tin is all you have to worry about."

I came very close to showing my surprise. There was only one answer to such a description of our intended cargo.

Narcotics.

"What's in it for us?" I demanded.

"Well, it isn't much of a job. All you have to do is bring it back here and I'll pick it up. Let's say five hundred bucks."

Looking at Carling, I nodded with seeming satisfaction over the price. Carling appeared pleased, too.

"Righto," he agreed. "Will do."

After Ellingsworth had gone, I sat there drumming my fingers on the desk in Carling's office, turning the whole plan over in my mind. Something, somewhere, didn't seem quite right.

Later I called McDaniels and he was for springing the trap immediately.

"Take along a soldering iron and open the box before you land," he directed. "If it is narcotics, as you suspect, we'll get the ship and we'll have other agents hidden near the hangar. You can give a signal and we'll close in and take Ellingsworth after he accepts the tin from you."

"And if it isn't?"

"What do you mean?"

"I'm not quite certain," I admitted. "But something smells pretty fishy to me in the whole setup. In the first place, why would he trust us so casually with narcotics worth a fortune? And why would he accept delivery so openly? It stinks. I've got a hunch we should go through with this delivery as scheduled and let it develop from there."

Reluctant to delay, McDaniels finally consented to play it my way.

Thus, following the arrangements made with Ellingsworth, two days after our meeting Carling and I took off and flew due south. And, as the chief petty officer had told us, hove to in a flat calm was the Alhambra. We sat the plane afloat, taxied near the ship and immediately her captain came out in a small boat and handed up a package wrapped carelessly in a piece of gunnysack.

Flying back, I unwrapped the burlap and there was the tin, sealed with expert smoothness. Weighing it thoughtfully in my hand, I knew I was taking a big chance handing it over to Ellingsworth without making an arrest.

We had rewrapped the tin in the burlap sacking and, when we handed it to Ellingsworth in Carling's office, the chief petty officer sat it on the desk and paused to fix us with a long, searching look.

"Got a soldering iron?" he asked.

Carling produced one and the chief, after unwrapping

the tin and scanning the seal minutely, bobbed his head in satisfaction. Then, to our surprise, he took the soldering iron, which had been heating, and melted off the sealing metal. Throwing open the lid, he withdrew a packet, opened it with a dramatic gesture and held it out to us.

"Wet your finger and taste it!" he commanded.

We did, and looked at each other in surprise.

"I say . . ." Carling bit off.

"Sugar," I raised my eyebrows inquiringly. "What's this all about?"

Ellingsworth laughed boisterously.

"You boys came through with flying colors. After all, we had to make sure you wouldn't hijack us completely, try to dip into the contents or turn us in. We had a dry run because this is a half million dollar deal, boys, and we don't take chances."

Trying to appear indignant, I growled, "What's the matter? Didn't you ever hear of honor among thieves?"

Ellingsworth laughed again, highly pleased with himself.

"Maybe the laugh's on you," I said. "We'll take that five hundred bucks, which makes it a damned expensive sugar shipment in this town."

The chief petty officer still was chuckling over his imagined cleverness while counting out the five hundred dollars. Then he sobered.

"Okay. Tomorrow we go for real."

Taking a road map from his pocket, he spread it out on the desk. It was, I saw, a detailed map of Louisiana and Arkansas.

"Now," Ellingsworth got down to business, "tomorrow you'll make the Alhambra just like today. She'll be laying over in the same spot. But instead of bringing the cargo back here to me, here's what you do."

He flattened out the map carefully.

"Follow the Mississippi up here just past the Arkansas border," he directed, tracing the route with a stubby forefinger. "Now right here, a couple miles back from the river, you'll see a good-sized lake. On the south shore you'll see a cleared field marked by a T-shaped landing strip. There'll be a plane there. You just run up near the shore, hand the tin over to a big guy wearing a green jacket, and your job is done."

"Not quite," I shook my head. "How much?"

Ellingsworth smiled shortly.

"A thousand bucks."

I wiped the grin off his face.

"No good. We want fifteen hundred, half in advance."

He stared hard at me, started to say something, then nodded.

"All right. But you'll have to settle for five hundred now. It's all I got. The big boss, the guy in the green jacket, will pay you the balance."

Later, after Ellingsworth had gone, I handed over the money to the appreciative Carling and then got in touch with McDaniels.

"Lucky we played it the way we did," he said when I told him what had happened.

"Uh huh," I agreed, and we then laid out our plans for the next day.

McDaniels was to make hush-hush arrangements for a Coast Guard cutter to intercept the Alhambra on a wing-dipping signal from us that we had picked up the cargo. Arrangements also were made to have narcotics agents apprehend Ellingsworth and for others to be waiting in the vicinity of the airfield, ready to close in once we sat down on the lake.

"You'll see our cars parked on the road leading in from the lake," McDaniels concluded. "They'll move in when they see your plane starting down."

That night I met Celeste and told her I thought I'd be moving on shortly.

"I am sorry," she said in her soft, slurring voice. "I'll have to find another room."

"You don't have a room of your own?" I asked in surprise.

"Of course. I have your room. Now I will find another. Why should I waste money on one I don't use? I have a little suitcase. That is my real private room. The others, most times, don't really matter."

It beat me. And yet, she was so immaculately clean, so refreshingly unspoiled, so much a sweet, warm woman, that I never ceased to marvel at her.

The next day was almost an anticlimax, almost but not quite, as the early part of our business went off like clockwork. We landed near the Alhambra with the gulf still slick and untroubled, took aboard another tin wrapped in burlap from the smiling ship's captain, and soaring aloft soon spotted the cutter. Waggling our wings, we saw the foam purl from the cutter's bow as she leaped toward the distant Alhambra.

Soon afterwards we were following the Mississippi northward, carefully tracing our course on the map, and eventually Carling located off to our left the lake we were seeking. Gliding through a full turn, we located the air strip and saw that the plane was waiting.

"Bank over toward the road," I told Carling. "I want to check if the cars are in position."

To my dismay, there were no automobiles parked along its length. Then in the distance I observed two cars leaving a trail of dust in their wake as they raced toward the airfield. They still were too far off for comfort and I figured quickly that if I didn't stall off the unknown boss waiting below, the agents would be too late to be of much help. Yet, we couldn't delay aloft without arousing suspicion.

"Set her down, but cut the engine when you're about fifty yards from shore as if it stalled," I ordered Carling. "I'll pole her in."

But the man in the green coat, standing on the bank as expected, didn't waste time waiting when our motor cut out. He leaped into a rowboat and rowed rapidly toward us. He was, I saw when he came closer, a sandy-haired giant with a hooked nose and a cleft chin. And he was decidedly impatient.

"Hey, you," he rumbled. "Toss it over and let's get the hell out of here."

"Not so fast," I told him as the rowboat bumped one of the pontoons. "We got a thousand bucks coming. I'll go along to shore with you and collect."

Holding the tin carefully under my arm, I scrambled into the rowboat. The big man spun it around like a toy and sent it scudding over the water until it ground ashore.

"Okay," he snapped. "I'll take it now."

"The thousand?" I reminded.

Reaching into his pocket, he pulled out a roll of bills and carelessly peeled off ten one hundred dollar bills. While he was doing it, I scanned the borders of the field but no help seemed materializing as yet.

"Now gimme that box," he ordered, handing over the money.

There was only one thing to do, because I knew if he ever reached that plane we had lost him. I pulled my .38 from my hip pocket and covered him.

"Federal agent," I announced. "Put 'em . . ."

That was as far as I got. Never have I seen a big man move with such lightning speed. The tin flew out of his hands and crashed into my gun, knocking it from my hand. Then he hit me a wallop that spun me ten feet out into the water.

I almost blacked out but the dousing cleared my head. Scrambling out of the lake and picking up my .38, I saw him running across the field to his plane. Racing after him, I was still twenty yards away when his prop ticked over, the engine roared to life and the plane slowly began to roll.

I always loved airplanes and I hated to do it. But sighting carefully, I emptied my .38 into the engine and sighed with relief as it sputtered and died. My satisfaction was short-lived, however, for now, with my pistol empty, the enraged behemoth had leaped from the cockpit and was bearing down on me with murder in his eyes.

At that moment, the agents who had been delayed by taking a wrong turn, arrived on the scene just like the United States Cavalry in a shoot 'em up serial. They drove right out on the strip and the frustrated man mountain just stood there with his ham-like hands hanging at his sides as they piled out of their cars and enveloped him.

It ended, McDaniels told me happily, with a clean sweep of all concerned and we had broken up one of the largest narcotics operations in the country.

That night, with a train ticket for the morrow's Chicago express in my pocket, I sat a last time in the speakeasy run by Carling's friend. All the goodbyes were over, except for Celeste sitting across from me a bit more quiescent than usual.

Then, too soon, it was the next afternoon and I had a train to catch.

"See, now it is nobody's room again," Celeste murmured, standing with her tiny bag in hand and gazing around at the room while I snapped the catch on my suitcase.

I took out a wad of bills and walked toward her.

"It's still your room," I told her. "I want you to take this money, Celeste. It will keep you here quite a while."

Gently she pushed the money back at me, hurt showing in her liquid eyes.

"I told you I need no room of my own. Besides, Paul, I would not take money from you. We have meant too much to each other."

She paused and her voice was barely audible.

"Do this for me, Paul. Just stay here a few moments until I have gone."

Celeste reached up and kissed me tenderly. Then the door closed behind her.

A very unusual woman, I reflected longingly as the train thundered through the night toward Chicago.

CHAPTER 16

The assignment in New Orleans had been a refreshing change of pace and yet it was good to get back to Chicago in plenty of time for the impending windup. The squad still was on the prowl for any new beer or liquor operations the mob might have installed but the tenor of the times was summed up succinctly by Leeson after a series of fruitless nights.

"I feel," he grunted with patent disgust, "about as necessary around here any more as flannel underwear at a nudists' convention."

We kept trying, though, and by sheer observation after a dry spell of almost a month finally nailed a load.

It began when we were driving down to the Loop and stopped for a light immediately in back of an open-end moving van. Protruding from the rear was a rather ornate baby grand piano with some other articles of furniture visible just beyond it.

"Take a gander at the carving on those piano legs," I commented idly.

"Class," Leeson noted. "Real class."

We were in the same neighborhood the next day when a truck rumbled across an intersection at which we were stopped and I caught a fragmentary glimpse of its rear end.

"Hey," I told Joe with some surprise, "there goes that same moving van we saw yesterday and I'll be damned if it isn't carrying that same piano."

"You're nutty," Leeson analyzed.

"For a dollar?"

"You're on."

Turning the corner, I speeded up and soon overhauled the van. I was right. Sticking out of the rear just as before was the same piano. There was no mistaking those curiously carved legs.

"Something's screwy here," Joe frowned. "Let's trail this dude to wherever he's going."

Dropping back to avert suspicion, we followed the truck until it turned in at a warehouse whose sign advertised moving and storage. The large double doors closed behind the truck but, after we parked nearby, we found a small door at the side which was unlocked.

Walking quietly inside, we went completely unobserved as we stood amid a welter of stored furniture and watched the men in moving-company overalls grunt and groan while they lowered our fancy piano to the floor. Out came a few more pieces of furniture, exposing what turned out to be fifty cases of imported whiskey.

"We'll stack it under those rugs in the corner along with the other stuff," one of the men directed. Then he looked up and his mouth dropped open when he saw us watching them.

"What the hell . . .?" he blurted.

"Oh, it's all right," Joe commented mildly. "We're only prohibition agents."

All three looked as if they might burst into tears.

Nearby, covered by a pile of stored rugs, we found two hundred more cases of whiskey. We made them load the truck and then, as we prepared to take it and them down to the office, one of the men savagely upended the piano, which crashed over on its side with a jangling of chords.

"God damnit," he growled, "I'm so sick and tired of carrying that piano around I'm glad we got caught. The bastard would have given me a hernia in another week."

Later, on our way home, I held out my hand, palm up.

"The buck," I demanded.

Dolefully he handed it over with a mock groan.

"You put me to work," he complained, "and I have to pay you for it. That's real robbery."

It wasn't long thereafter that Capone went on trial and it was a three-ring circus which, even at its opening, began on a disastrous note for the mob.

The very first day, when the trial recessed for lunch, I started walking out of the courtroom with the crowd when I was jostled roughly from behind. Looking over my shoulder, I observed that it was Phil D'Andrea, Capone's chief bodyguard and the same hoodlum who had led the lobby guard the day Leeson and I invaded the Lexington Hotel to needle the mob in its own headquarters.

The crowd was thick and there was a great deal of pushing and shoving but when D'Andrea jostled me arrogantly a second time I jammed backwards with my elbow just to warn him to keep his distance. But I was surprised when my elbow struck something hard and unyielding.

There was no question in my mind. D'Andrea was packing a shoulder-holstered pistol right in a federal courtroom.

Before the trial resumed after the luncheon break, I informed a United States marshal whom I knew about the incident. He disappeared for a few minutes and then I was summoned into Judge Wilkerson's chambers.

"The marshal advised me what you suspect," the jurist said. "Are you certain of this?"

"Positive, your honor."

"Well," Wilkerson was grim, "you point him out and he'll regret his actions in this court."

When court resumed, D'Andrea walked boldly into the room and, pushing his way through the railing, took a seat at the defense table. The judge beckoned me to the bench and, when I pointed out D'Andrea to him, ordered the marshals to escort the mobster forward.

"See if this man is carrying a pistol," Wilkerson ordered.

D'Andrea was.

"That will cost you six months for contempt of court," the judge pronounced icily. "Take him away and let that be a lesson to anyone else who thinks he can take this court lightly."

There was a great deal of looking at the floor and the ceiling by various members of the mob in attendance and several of them rose and hurried from the room.

The lurid details of the Capone trial need no repeating, being a well-chronicled part of criminal jurisprudence. Suffice it to say for the record that "Scarface Al" was convicted on October 24, 1931, fined $50,000 and sentenced to eleven years in prison. There were six months of appeals but the verdict finally stood.

On May 3, 1932, our entire squad was on hand to accompany the one-time terror of the underworld from the Cook County jail to the Dearborn Station, where we saw him stowed safely aboard the Dixie Flyer for his trip to the Atlanta Penitentiary.

It marked the beginning of the end for the Untouchables because first one and then another was reassigned to other districts.

Froelich left at the end of May and now only Leeson and I remained in Chicago on special assignment, doing what Froelich called "mop-up duty."

The last seizure that Leeson and I made together was fully illustrative of the depths to which the mob had sunk financially.

We were driving through a South Side alley, and I have thought often that it was for both of us simply an unplanned journey down memory lane, when we were held up by a slow-moving truck loaded with cabbage.

"What the hell is it?" Joe wrinkled his nose.

"Cabbage."

"Yeah, I know. But what the hell's wrong with it?"

"It sure does smell rotten," I agreed.

Raucously blowing our horn, we finally were able to squeeze past.

"Hey, pull up," Joe told me suddenly. "The two guys in that truck aren't dressed like farmers, produce merchants, garbage men or whatever in the hell they're supposed to be. Let's take a look."

We stopped our car, effectively blocking the alley, and

now the truck driver began to lean on his horn. We got out and walked back to them.

"Okay, knock it off," Joe ordered. "Where are you guys going with that load of garbage?"

"Who the hell are you?" asked the driver.

"Federal agents," I replied.

Their reaction was indicative of the sorry state into which we had driven Chicago bootlegging. They didn't even try a bluff.

"All right," the one beside the driver shrugged resignedly. "So we got a few cases of whiskey."

We made them drive to the city dump and then stood off at a safe nasal distance while, swearing lividly, they shoveled off the offensive cabbage. Underneath were thirty cases of liquor and we added injury to insult by making them methodically smash every bottle. Then we locked them up.

The last thing I heard out of them was one saying to the other:

"Ya damned fool, I told ya we shouldda bought some fresh cabbage instead of trying to use it again."

"What," the other asked plaintively, "did you expect me to use for money?"

Such, by now, was the shape of the one-time multi-million dollar bootlegging racket in Chicago.

Time began to drag more and more heavily on our hands and it got even worse for me when Leeson received orders in July of 1932 to report to Kansas City.

"I sure hate to leave you behind, Paul," he told me when, on his last night, we broke open a bottle of misplaced evidence. "Here's to you, the last remaining member of 'The Untouchables.' "

"You big ape," I managed over the lump in my throat, "I'll be glad to see the last of your ugly kisser."

Both of us had economy-sized hangovers when I put him on the train the next morning. And I felt even worse when Joe crushed my hand in his, spun on his heel with a muffled "So long," and plunged aboard. I felt like the last chili bean in the bottom of an empty pot.

After Joe left, the days and weeks really began to crawl past and it was as if I was living in a vacuum. My heart leaped when, in late August, I received a letter in Mavis' familiar handwriting.

It was, however, a disappointingly short note.

Dear Paul:

Reports we get out here in sleepy Iowa are that Chicago is really closed down tight. Jack didn't stay here very long. He's in Kansas City and, I'm afraid, living on the shady side again. He told me in a letter that he heard Cermak may take a little ride.

All is well with me and I hope it is with you, too.

Mavis.

My eyes kept going back to that one line about Cermak. For Anton Cermak had been elected mayor of Chicago in April of 1931 as a "wet" candidate and a supposed choice of the underworld. Since his election, however, he had moved vigorously against the mobs and the whispers were that the syndicate might strike even this high in deadly reprisal.

I didn't put much stock in what Mavis relayed from Jack. Not at this time. After all, I reasoned, we had hit the mob harder than anyone and, confessing to a great deal of luck, had lived through it.

Feeling as if I was a mere spectator on the Chicago scene, I watched closely from the sidelines when in December of 1932 one of Mayor Cermak's newly-created gangster squads raided the syndicate headquarters on North La Salle Street. The squad was headed by Detective Sergeants Harry Lang and Harry Miller.

Nitti, who had moved up as business manager of the Capone mob, was shot three times by Lang but, despite expectations, did not die.

Word was whispered about, and I heard it from a stoolie we had used on occasion, that a gangster named Ted Newberry had offered $15,000 to have Nitti rubbed out. And Newberry reputedly was on comradely terms with north side Democrats who had backed Cermak.

The rumors were fatal for Newberry. About three

weeks after Nitti was shot, Newberry's body was found in an Indiana ditch, riddled with shotgun slugs.

The subsequent trials of Nitti and Lang may have cost Cermak his life.

Nitti was charged with assault with intent to kill the arresting Lang, who said he fired in self defense. But one of the raiders testified that Nitti was unarmed and did not resist arrest.

He also testified that before the raid, Lang had stopped in Cermak's office for instructions.

Five and one-half months after I received Mavis' note, Cermak was slain on February 15, 1933, while standing beside President-elect Franklin D. Roosevelt at a Miami reception.

The assassin, an unemployed bricklayer named Joe Zangara, testified that he was trying to kill Roosevelt.

It was a remarkable miss, considering that Zangara had been a crack marksman in the Italian army.

Zangara, who was speedily tried and convicted, died in the electric chair two weeks after Cermak's death.

With him went the answer to how he, unemployed by his own word for three years, had lived in Miami during the height of the resort season for six weeks and in the three days prior to the shooting had dropped $200 at the dog races.

I recalled that phrase in Mavis' letter that Jack Martin "heard Cermak may take a little ride."

There was no question in my mind.

Zangara was a Mafia killer. He had been sent to Miami for the express purpose of eradicating Cermak.

Then it was Omerta, the law of silence to the death which we also had encountered.

Shortly after the Cermak slaying, I applied for transfer to another district.

"There's a great deal of smuggling off the Florida and Georgia coast," I was told. "How would you like an assignment to Jacksonville?"

I jumped at it. Chicago held too many memories and too little action.

As Chicago fell behind me I stopped my car and looked back for one last view of the skyline. Considering Cermak's fate, which I felt unquestionably had been ordained by the mob, I mused that we had been more than lucky. It had been quite a town and quite an assignment.

Then I turned, put the car in gear and headed for Jacksonville.

EPILOGUE

Paul Robsky's violent, action-packed career did not end when he was the last of "The Untouchables" to leave Chicago.

For almost a year after his departure from the one-time Capone stronghold he had helped to smash, Robsky pursued smugglers running in whiskey from the Bahamas and other liquor violators in Jacksonville, Florida; Charleston, South Carolina, and Savannah, Georgia.

When the repeal of Prohibition in December of 1933 spelled the demise of the Prohibition Bureau, he became a special investigator for the Alcohol Tax Unit, Bureau of Internal Revenue.

Robsky played a leading role in 1936 in the "Hillfern Case," the last involving the smuggling into the United States of foreign manufactured alcohol. Through his efforts the government thwarted a syndicate plan to illegally import 180,000 gallons of alcohol in the British motorship *Hillfern* in a multi-million dollar underworld deal.

At Augusta, Georgia, Robsky seized a boxcar of whiskey being illegally shipped into a dry state in what was famed as the "Reo Distillers Case." This resulted in revision of treasury department regulations for distilleries and drove the underworld from the legitimate end of the liquor business.

Robsky was one of the first investigators on hand at the Amagansett spy landings from a submarine laying off Long Island, which was believed, at first, to be a smuggling operation.

Retiring from federal service in April of 1951, Robsky

engaged in private investigative work. Today, happily married, he is a security agent for the Wackenhut Corp. and few people recognize this trim, quiet man as "the last of The Untouchables."

—Oscar Fraley

Bullet-Riddled Novels Of Crime And Mob Power . . . And The Men Who Stand For Law And Order!

THE LUCIANO STORY Feder and Joesten
The true story of Lucky Luciano—the most feared crime boss of them all. "A tale to make the blood run colder than any fiction!—**New Hampshire News.** AR1457—$1.75

THE DON Forrest V. Perrin
Gangland explodes with raw fury as an aging Godfather's crime empire crumbles into dust. AN1083—95¢

UNLESS THEY KILL ME FIRST Vincent Siciliano
A former mobster reveals the true, inside story of today's rackets. "A long-fused bomb which readers ought to be warned will be hard to put down."—**Publishers Weekly.** AN0748—95¢

THUNDERBOLT AND LIGHTFOOT Joe Millard
Clint Eastwood stars in the action-packed film about the most fantastic heist since "The Sting." The novel captures all the slam-bang excitement and suspense. AQ1465—$1.25

BADGE 373 Mike Roote
A cop without a gun—alone against a ruthless drug syndicate! The blockbuster sequel to "The French Connection!"
AN1164—95¢

THE UNTOUCHABLES Eliot Ness with Oscar Fraley
The brutal story of the battle against "Scarface" Al Capone. The explosive book that triggered the famous TV series. "Hair-raising!"—**Los Angeles Times.** AD1484—$1.50

THE STONE KILLER John Gardner
Charles Bronson stars in the blistering motion picture about a tough cop on a one-man war of vengeance. "A superior crime story with a superior hero."—**New Yorker.** AQ1181—$1.25

THE NICKEL RIDE Michael T. Kaufman
A chilling novel of fear and death in today's changing urban underworld. AQ1351—$1.25

USE HANDY, MONEY-SAVING ORDER FORM ON BACK PAGE